MW00581899

THE ELITE BICYCLE

Portraits of great marques,
makers and designers

Gerard Brown and Graeme Fife

FOREWORD BY SIR PAUL SMITH

THE ELITE BICYCLE

Portraits of great marques, makers and designers

Copyright © 2013 photographs by Gerard Brown
Copyright © 2013 text by Graeme Fife
Copyright © 2013 photograph of Paul Smith by Alistair Strong

3002 Sterling Circle, Suite 100
Boulder, Colorado 80301-2338 USA
(303) 440-0601 • Fax (303) 444-6788
E-mail velopress@competitorgroup.com

Distributed in the United States and Canada
by Ingram Publisher Services.

For information on purchasing VeloPress books,
please call (800) 811-4210, ext. 2138,
or visit www.velopress.com.

ISBN 978-1-937715-08-3

A CIP record for this book is available from the Library of
Congress.

All rights reserved. No part of this publication may
be reproduced or used in any form or by any means
– photographic, electronic or mechanical, including
photocopying, recording, taping or information storage or
retrieval systems – without permission of the publishers.

This book is produced using paper that is made from wood
grown in managed sustainable forests. It is natural, renewable
and recyclable. The logging and manufacturing processes
conform to the environmental regulations of the country of
origin.

Design by XAB Design
Printed in China by C&C
10 9 8 7 6 5 4 3 2 1

CONTENTS

FOREWORD

In a world which is filled with too much of 'everything' it has never been more important to be making things by hand by artisans and specialists. Having a craft is so crucial. Unfortunately, over the last 25 years the obsession with mass production, expansion and greed has been prolific. This wonderful book, *The Elite Bicycle*, really celebrates the passion of people who are still content to make things, in small quantities, by hand. I'm really proud of the people in this book. They are real craftsmen. It's about an attitude and state of mind and this book celebrates this state of mind.

SIR PAUL SMITH

INTRODUCTION

The modern bicycle can, thanks to the availability of a rich variety of frames and components, be adapted to the needs and purposes of many different types of cyclist: for sport, (on road, track, country), commuting, touring, modest excursion … for pleasure, for leisure as well as for extreme levels of athletic discipline.

The diversity of bicycle manufacture reflects the burgeoning popularity of and interest in a machine whose essential design has not changed since its invention. At one end of the spectrum, the Asian mass production factories, relatively new on the scene, have brought efficient and enjoyable cycling to millions at very reasonable prices. At the other end, the specialist market and the individual constructeur who makes or builds one bicycle specifically for one buyer at a time. There is, too, the larger specialist enterprise, the hi-tech operation which applies aerospace engineering and production methods and quality. They, as all the people included here, compromise neither on materials nor technical values in the making of what they consider to be the best bicycle that can be made. Today's cyclists are fortunate indeed to have their needs and wants supplied by such a large and diverse industry dedicated to their safety and comfort and performance.

Elite identifies the very best, and the following series of profiles is a snapshot of the top end of the bicycle production industry, focusing on 29 companies which merit that epithet. The selection is not comprehensive. It is, rather, a portrait of a small cadre of exceptional makers and enterprises which combine traditional craftsmanship and new technology in the manufacture of the essential component parts of a bicycle. From the production of a 500g leather saddle which hasn't changed for almost a century, to the fashioning of a carbon-fibre frame which weighs a mere 800g. Nor is élite the monopoly of professional racing. Superlative materials and technology have been applied to every facet of cycling.

The people we've met in the course of researching this book, all highly-skilled exponents of their respective crafts, are dedicated and passionate men and women who understand the value, and not simply the price, of what they produce. Quality before cost. We felt that these craftsmen, artists and engineers should be celebrated more widely and generously. They fuse traditional values with a constant thirst for innovation. Steel, for example, once the darling of the bicycle industry but long since overtaken by

aluminium, carbon and titanium, is being used again, with superior modern production methods, and thus introduced to a new generation. HG Wells said 'Every time I see an adult on a bicycle, I no longer despair for the future of the human race.'

Now we may add to that sentiment, with a flourish and delight, children. Here, then, are men and women who, in workshops small and large, with hand tools and machines, celebrate and grace the culture of the bicycle and impart to it a singular dose of their enthusiasm, intellectual and manual brilliance, their creative drive and devotion to the making of the élite bicycle.

Gerard Brown
Graeme Fife

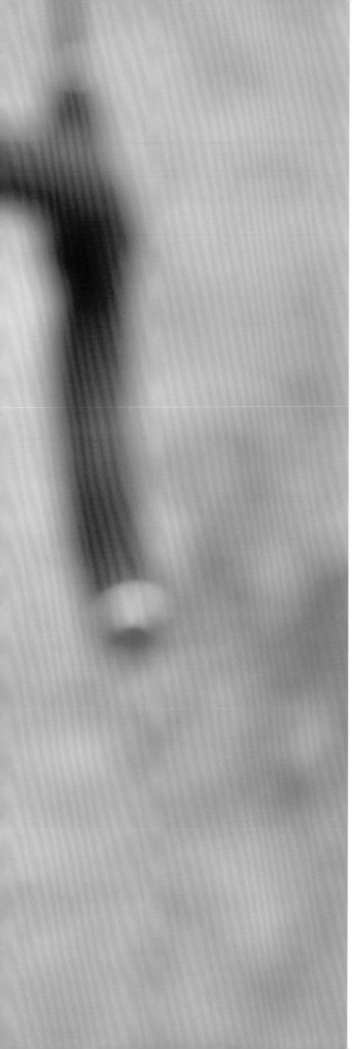

SADDLES • Smethwick, West Midlands, UK

Brooks now make a wide range of leather goods as well as saddles: bar tape, toolbags, trouser bands and other items, all manufactured economically from off-cuts.

BROOKS

In 1865, a harness-maker, John Boultbee Brooks, with, reputedly, £20 in his pocket, left his native Leicestershire town of Hinckley for Birmingham. He established a business in horse harnesses and general leather goods in Great Charles Street under the name JB Brooks & Co. and rode to and from the works on his horse. In 1878, his faithful old horse died and because, it's said, he could not afford (or, perhaps choose) to replace the beloved steed, he accepted the loan of a friend's bicycle, a machine that was, at the time, dubbed 'the horse that eats no hay'. It was fitted with a wooden saddle. Brooks found the wretched thing so excruciatingly uncomfortable* that he resolved to make a seat as lenient as that which he'd enjoyed on the horse which did eat hay. On 28 October 1882, his first patent – Saddles for Bicycles and Tricycles – launched the manufacture of what became, until the 1950s, the best selling saddle in the world. The company's first logo shows a bee with outspread wings beneath a single word – Industria. This may be glossed 'Busy as a bee'.

Brooks applied the expertise of making equine saddles to a comfy seat for the new-fangled machine, in particular, the moulding of thick cow leather to the form of the human buttocks. The process he evolved is still in use and one of the saddles, the B17 model, first included in the 1890s Brooks catalogue, is still being sold, billed originally, as now, as 'a neat saddle

---

* Ghenghis Khan insisted that his Mongol cavalry ride angular wooden saddles as a constant reminder that their job was ruthless conquest, not comfort. I can vouch personally for the efficacy of the Khan's message.

The 5mm thick hides have to be soaked in water to make them pliable enough to work.

Stiff sheets of leather sit in the warehouse awaiting selection and working.

Immense pressure forces the rawhide blanks into the smooth flowing moulds.

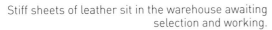

Having been cut to the correct shape the leather awaits 'the process'.

Most of the machinery required to make a Brooks saddle is old, heavy and noisy. The physics of this sort of manufacture demands both precision and force; lightweight doesn't get a look in.

TOP LEFT
The moulded leather is trimmed with a knife before the saddle shapes are gently oven-dried.

ABOVE
As they await the process of fixing them to the frame, the saddle tops have an alluring sensual quality. They're hard, shiny and the form flows beautifully along the length.

LEFT
Every Brooks saddle passes through up to a dozen pairs of hands before leaving the factory.

Champfering requires the cutting skills of a bespoke tailor, the eye of a watchmaker and the precision of a micro-engineer. A mere slip can ruin a Brooks saddle. That such a delicate procedure comes almost at the end of the production process means that a very experienced hand is required. Eric Murray has such a hand.

of best quality'. Indeed, the whole ethos of the Brooks operation – and it extends beyond saddles* – is very old-school, even slightly antiquated. Yet, when the present Works Manager arrived in 1999 and decided that he needed to bring this renowned company 'not just into the 21st century but into the 20th century', he discovered that the traditional methods of manufacture are just right for Brooks. Change has no intrinsic virtue and the first aim remains the principal aim – 'to use the best materials, designs and construction that experience, skill and money can procure'.

The saddle leather, 5mm thick, is cut from the butt (rump) of a cow and grease dressed to render it practically waterproof but capable of breathing. Thus it will not get clammy from a sweaty bottom in hot weather. The rear end of the butt is harder and goes to the racing saddle, the belly is softer and serves other models. In the three days it takes to produce a Brooks saddle, the shapes are cut from the hide – and very little is wasted, the

interstices are made into washers – soaked for an hour in water, drip dried and given the first moulding while still damp. This process combines a mechanical press and the skilled hands of a Trimmer. Next to the trimmer's table, a hand-written placard: Qualifications for being a Trimmer: Grip like a Vice, Strength of a 800lb Gorilla, Stamina of a Viking rower.

The moulded leather, dried in two different ovens at different temperatures for a further two hours, passes to the next procedure: the fitting of the frame. Boultbee Brooks' introduction of the coiled spring (a comparatively recent development) into the making of his saddle was a stroke of genius. Early bicycles had all been fitted with solid seats as unforgiving as the solid tyres. The marriage of moulded leather to a sub-frame supported on a strong spring which gave slightly under the pressure of bumps in the road suddenly turned the bicycle into a quite different machine.

The Brooks frame and springs come from the steel or titanium wire which arrives at the Smethwick works wrapped round big drums, and are

* They also designed satchels, knapsacks, golf bags, tea and picnic cases, tool pouches, car trunks, even a punch bag.

fabricated in-house on two splendid old bits of factory equipment – one, a 1954 German machine, produces the left spring, the other, British, 1949, the right spring. Thus, after the terrible conflict of WWII, Germany and Great Britain were united 'neath the behinds of every cyclist mounted on a Brooks. If this sounds whimsical, it does pertain very much to the deliberately classical mindset of the Brooks operation, as evinced in the stamping of their name on either flap of the saddle and the tiny plaque affixed to its rear. 'Warning [says the early publicity and the continuing belief]. It is as well to be assured that the saddle you buy as a Brooks bears the name ... on the flaps and at the rear; it may save you considerable disappointment.' The fact is, many professional cyclists of the post-war era – Merckx, Simpson, Coppi et al – rode Brooks saddles and kept them to put on the new frame when they changed. A Brooks was a precious item, not only because it did its job to perfection, but because it moulded itself to its rider. That remains part of its current appeal – not only the very 'in' retro look – but the way it shapes itself to its owner. And, the final process of manufacture for the racing model,

the champfering of the edges, a very tricky operation which risks ruining the whole saddle, is further earnest of the care that goes into the Brooks.

It even contributed to cyclist's slang. 'On the rivet' means 'flat out, full gas' and refers to the large copper rivet which fixes the slim nose of the sleek top-of-the-range racing Brooks to its narrow frame. The ordinary range models are fixed with tubular rivets although both have an adjusting nut at the fore end to tighten the leather when, with use, it begins to lose any tension. The handsome smooth copper medallion set in the glossy hide is a distinctive badge of class.

Although the Brooks enterprise evinces a certain old-fashioned image, it is far from being fuddy-duddy. A collaboration with students from the Royal College of Arts in London – 'the most influential, wholly postgraduate university of art and design in the world' – stimulates that very innovation and entrepreneurial drive for which Brooks' founder is rightly celebrated.

Eric Murray is a safe pair of hands.

Fitting rivets and attaching the saddle top to the frame.

The spot-welding press: an electric current fixes the two parts of the wire frame together. Managed properly the process is quick, efficient and strong. Bag loops are incorporated into some designs such as the Swift.

An experienced eye gives a visual check. Two hoppers filled with different components arrive at this workstation. Before long, the newly joined metal elements leave as one item.

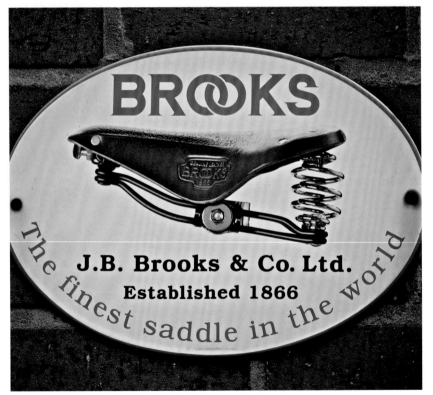

Hammering these beautiful copper rivets requires a steady hand and a trained eye. The idea is to flatten the head sufficiently to spread the load across as wide a surface as possible whilst keeping both surfaces flush.

SELLE ITALIA

Corsico, now a large commune (in 1987, declared an honorary city), outside Milan, was, in 1897, no more than a village when it became home to a new industrial enterprise: Selle Italia. Taking its cue from the emergence of a verifiable Italian identity, for the first time after many centuries of foreign rule and civic disintegration, the new company adopted as its motto ITALIA INVINCIBILE. If the political thrust of that message proved wobbly, the Selle Italia end did not. They have stayed in the saddle, so to put it, ever since.

In the small museum at the headquarters in a large modern complex of buildings at Asolo, west of Treviso, stand four antique machines, the core of the original production process: a Singer sewing machine of the early 1900s*; a bending drum press (*pressa piega fusti*) for shaping the rods for the saddle's base, worked by hydraulic power; the *timbratrice* for stamping each saddle with the company's name and brand (*timbra*); and a Marelli hydraulic pump of 1891, which transfers generating power by way of a thick canvas drive band. That's it, technology in place, out come the saddles. Well, not exactly. Every single model of Selle Italia that has reached and still reaches the market has been worked, at least in part, by hand. Curiously, the company still looks to its humble bucolic origins. When we ask Ingrid Bordignon, who welcomes us, where the production happens, she tells us that it's in the hands of a scattered array of outworkers – small family operations, men and women working in their spare time, perhaps, combining this labour with secondary part-time work. As a former manager of a tiny cottage industry which produced goods to sell in an international market, I warm to this. I once took one of our principal American buyers on a visit, to collect

*The first hand-operated sewing machine was actually invented by Elias Howe. His fellow American, Isaac Merrit Singer, proved to be more adept at development and marketing.

23

an assignment from one of our best outworkers at her house in a remote Norfolk village. He, a resident of Manhattan, was at once astonished, delighted, dumbfounded, speechless. Real homespun.

So, it still goes on. The Selle Italia satellites produce some 9,600 handmade saddles every day. Every day. Two million per annum. Materials ferried by a posse of cars and vans to the workers, finished bits back to the plant. But what about quality control? How can such a large enterprise as Selle Italia keep tabs on such a disparate workforce? The answer is nebulous but the proof is that the product sells and people don't complain. When Viola Nardi, our designated guide, arrives – she's been delayed by a minor car accident – she conducts us to where we see one side, at least, of the meticulous attention and tight grip on manufacturing perfection for which the company is rightly famous.

In a laboratory in one corner of the capacious building which serves as warehouse, despatch area, cutting and assembly lines, and so on, we observe the rigorous testing of the prototype saddle, material, structure and assembly. The top surface of a saddle mounted on a seat pin, angles assured, is submitted to a constant pounding – a million strikes – by a hammer, 1000 newtons of pressure each time, for five days and nights. Not

quite the temptation in the wilderness but a very harsh, speeded up version of it. To the nosy question, 'Does the material ever break?', the answer is 'Yes, but very very rarely'. The materials undergo such tough examination all the way along the line before the saddle is assembled that final rupture is most unlikely. A prototype is, *ceteris paribus*, more or less guaranteed ready for sale but … it has its probation to serve. On another bench in the lab, an older machine tests the wear of friction on the seat – a moving pad of abrasive material rubs it back and forth, back and forth. Another contraption measures the exact height of the two saddle rails – a slight discrepancy will make the seat tilt and become uncomfortable and useless.

As we walk across to see how a compression machine bends the seat and then compresses the two rail ends into the nose slot, Viola expresses her enthusiasm. 'I was so proud when we won the Olympic road title with Vinokourov.' She's a cyclist, her grandfather was a semi-professional, riding is in the family blood. But why saddle manufacture in Treviso? Because, she says, cycling is and always has been so popular in this area. It boasts the largest percentage of cyclists, pro and amateur, leisure and workaday, in all of Italy. (Having taken a ride in Treviso city myself the night before, the streets much threaded by urban pedallers, I can vouch for its encouragement of the two wheels.)

LEFT
Every prototype saddle undergoes scrupulous testing before it is allowed to go into production.

ABOVE
The success of the product requires worldwide distribution.

RIGHT
The block, the mould and the basic shape of the most famous model, the 1982 Turbo.

The company vaunts its adherence to both tradition and innovation, lasting values, new ideas. (Most significantly, it introduced the use of gel in saddle manufacture.) Some while ago, it introduced its revolutionary system of IDMATCH which came out of lengthy research and development into the morphology of riders, male and female, and the way their body functions whilst riding. Ingrid tells the story of a dealer who, faced with what was a wildly cumbrous variety of some 90 available Selle Italia models, simply did not know where to start when advising customers what to buy. The new range comprises six sizes only, three large, three small. The determining factors for matching bum to seat are four: 1.) general parameters – age, height, weight, gender, type of cycling 2.) the outer distance (technically the interochanteric) measured between the crowns of the hips 3.) circumference of the thighs; 4.) angle of rotation of the pelvis when pushing the pedals. Based on an analysis of this data, Selle Italia will tell you what any individual's

ideal saddle will be. Comfort in the saddle is the vital role and it's the rotation of the pelvis that's key, not the flexibility of the back. Someone who can touch their toes with ease may actually have quite a limited pelvic rotation, and vice versa.

It seems all too simple, but complexity is often a blind for inaccuracy or confusion. Perhaps another part of the Selle Italia museum proves the worth of what they make quite as well as this sally into hi-tech computer mystery: the display cabinets housing saddles ridden by the many stars of the professional peloton, illustrious names which stand apart from many others, numerous others, who have ridden to victory on Selle Italia: Coppi, Merckx, Gimondi, Hinault, Pantani …

Not bad company to keep.

ABOVE
Every major race on the professional calendar has, at some point, been won on a Selle Italia saddle.

RIGHT
The styling is classic Italian, the manufacturing is outsourced. Families of subcontractors put the various parts of the saddle together before they come together at the factory for testing, quality control and packing.

REYNOLDS

The Reynolds company originally manufactured nails. As to how they proceeded from elementary wood fixings to their patent for butted tubing, I have my own idea, but it's probably not worth a small square of baco-foil – whose invention owes much to thoughtful contemplation of the thin paper used for hand-rolling cigarettes. A crucial application of intelligence, the capacity to draw analogy, often unlikely analogy.

Old Mr Reynolds set up his nail-making factory in 1848, the year when revolutions erupted across Europe. The Reynolds revolution didn't happen until 1897, when Alfred Reynolds, son of the founder of the nail foundry, took out a patent for butted tubing in conjunction with the company's Foreman. A year later, the Patent Butted Tube Co. Ltd was registered.

The technology of butted tubing may be explained thus. Butt, in this sense, may be connected with the French word *bout*, end, from *bouter*, to push out, and describes the thicker end of anything, such as the broad end of a spear shaft or the stock of a gun. Imagine a tube of uniform outer dimension, in which the inner dimension varies, so that it is thinner in the middle length, and thicker at both ends. The importance of thickness bears directly on strength, flexibility and lightness. The cleverness of the Reynolds process was to apply various characteristics of steel – its plasticity (its propensity to be worked into shape), its elasticity (how it may be stretched but how, once the stretch is released, the steel springs back), and its tensile and ductile qualities. Developments in the production of high grade steels accelerated during the 19th century. Once steel is forged, its molecular structure endows it with an intrinsic strength which the further application of heat will, by disturbing the molecules, impair. Therefore, cold working comes into play. Since the melting point of steel (depending on its grade) is between 1200 and 1400ºC, the epithet 'cold' denotes around 200–300ºC.

Enter the mandrel, which began life as a miner's pick and then became 'a cylindrical rod, core or axis, round which metal … is forged, cast, moulded or shaped'. [Oxford English Dictionary]. A shaping mandrel has tapered ends and is forced through plain (uniform) gauge tubing of a slightly narrower dimension than the mandrel. As the bulkier section of the mandrel clears the opening of the tube, the tube springs back to its starting size. (An analogy might be a bellows opening and closing.) The thicker mandrel now sits along the main central portion of the tube, its leading tapered end snug in the further end of the tube. Imagine a boa constrictor bulging with the shape of the prey it has just swallowed. The one end of the tube, which was only briefly stretched, retains its original thickness, the expanded portion is stretched to a new thinness. Here, then, is the new overall, varied thickness of the tube's final shape. But how to get the mandrel out? A machine called a reeler has offset rollers which place a lateral force on the tube as the tube containing the mandrel is pushed through them. By slightly expanding the hollow tube to make it just larger in diameter than the mandrel, the mandrel can be squeezed out, leaving the tube larger in diameter than at the start of the process. Imagine stretching a rubber band and then releasing it: it flies back to the original size. However, if the rubber is stretched beyond what's called the elastic limit (think tired knicker elastic, why not?), it remains as stretched. This is the case with the mandrel and reeler. The tube, now

Largely consigned to the history books and the boutique builder just a few years ago, top-quality steel tubing for top quality steel bicycles is now enjoying a well-deserved come back.

measuring larger in the middle than at either end, is thus butted. This is the process that Reynolds patented. Their mandrels are made from a heat-treated tool steel called D2, some of these have an additional nitride coating to reduce friction. They combine the use of these mandrels with specific lubricants depending on the material being drawn, in order to optimise the amount of cold work done at each stage.

Probably the most famous of the butted Reynolds tubing (the company took the more familiar name in 1924) is the 531 seamless manganese-molybdenum steel, with a 5-3-1 ratio of key elements, introduced in 1935. It was first used in aircraft manufacture for wing spars, strut and engine mountings, and later for sports car sub-frames and, of course, for bicycle frames. The 531 went into wartime Spitfires and Beaufort Fighters.

The chemistry of steel is an essential part of the Reynolds research and development, carried out in conjunction with metallurgists at the nearby University of Birmingham and at Carpenter in America. Development, improvement, a testing curiosity: the attributes of Reynolds from the outset. As Keith Noronha, the Managing Director put it: 'The most dangerous time for a company is when it is successful.' The search is constant for high grade steels with low carbon content which can be welded easily, materials that are light in weight but with a high resistance to fatiguing, and knowing how far to push the metal.

What, then, of titanium, that mineral discovered in Cornwall (but named by a German – for the Titans of legend) in the late 18th century? Strong, for sure, but the finest steel has a higher strength to weight ratio and the latest Reynolds tubing, the 953, is the most advanced material yet. Ultra light, very resilient, with a remarkably high impact strength, it uses Martensite steel, developed by Carpenter. Five years ago, Carpenter contacted Reynolds to say 'We have a great metal here – what can we do with it?' Bingo. 953.

The chemical ratios may actually not be as expressive of the various brands of Reynolds tubes as the more significant fact that 531, for example, can resist up to 53 tons per square inch before breaking … 753: 75 tons psi … 953 can hold out against 110 tons psi It's twenty-two times stronger than the original 531, stainless and virtually indestructible. Above all, it retains the feel of steel, that unique quality of flex to which more and more cyclists are returning or, newcomers, delighting in. Its origin? In the US military, for tanks, aircraft, ships. Purpose? To deflect Scud missiles. That strong. And, at the end of the Cold War, Russia sold off its massive stockpiles of titanium (also earmarked for the military) for more peaceable use. Hence the advent of titanium in bicycle manufacture.

A couple of the small workforce at the Birmingham factory have worked there for nearly four decades. They have a singular expertise which comes from close familiarity with the nature and quality of the material with which they work. In the process of swaging the tubes, for instance, Mario knows, through his fingertips, whether the metal is sound or not. The process involves a lot of hammer action and yet there's a shiver in the skilled man's hands which can detect the slightest flaw, from a sensitivity of touch born of long years of experience – the sort of experience that can only be learnt hands-on. And, walking the crowded shop floor, past the monsters of machinery, the grim-looking rollers, to the accompaniment of the thump and clack of various plant, one has a strong sense that the refined and refining work of craftsmen, complimentary to the extremely advanced science behind the composition of the materials used in Reynolds tubing, is a continuum of essential pleasure in making things the best they can be made.

Postscript: Why, (I hear you ask) does the logo for the 725 chrome-moly[bdenum] heat treated frame tubes have purple numbers? Apparently, as the design team were brainstorming, in came the refreshment tray bearing … a purple teapot.

Reynolds claim that their new 953 tubing takes steel alloy into a new league. They have created a super high strength stainless steel alloy which, some say, rivals titanium.

Seamless tubing is usually regarded as the best sort of tubing. It comes from a large billet of steel (Reynolds quote 10" x 36") which is heated to around 1000°C, rolled, drawn and pressed until it's about the right size for a bicycle tube.

Reynolds' labelling and naming have arcane origins but their gaudy little stickers, dating from early days, make a potent symbolism for the evolution of bicycle culture.

A lot of brute strength, sheer force and pressure goes into the manufacture of the thinnest and lightest steel tubing.

The seamless tubes are worked with mandrels and dies which determine both the inner and outer diameters. A staggering 50 tons psi of pressure is required to squeeze the tubing into the right shape.

TUBING • Milan, Italy

COLUMBUS

Against one side wall in Antonio Colombo's new and as yet unfurnished office in the complex of buildings which is now the home of Gruppo Cinelli Columbus lean paintings by Bukowski and Gabriello Aruzzo, covered in plastic sheeting, awaiting their place on display. Both artists delve with both flourish and humour into modern iconography, hinting at the intricate symbolism of early Renaissance art. Their presence in this room are testimony to Colombo's first love: art. He studied architecture, design, fine art. Not the obvious route for someone going into the business of metal tubing.

The company, trading as A.L. Colombo, was founded by his father Angelo Luigi in 1919. Why Columbus? An echo of the family name, but note the year when the machines started up – the conclusion of the Great War. Columbus is Latin for 'a male dove'. Once again, the theme of manufactured stuff turned from bellicose to peaceable purpose. The company made tubes of all kinds and, much influenced by the ascetic style of the Bauhaus, also the spare lines of tubing used for the support of various forms of furniture. The company produced chairs, tables and sideboards in the 1930s but stopped in the 1950s. The association of steel with war and the shortage of steel after war, another bloody war, deterred them.

Antonio himself became involved in 1972 … or 73. Was there pressure from his father? 'Oh, yes.' In his laconic response a hint at the scenario played out between them. But, Colombo is, and evidently was, firm on his own agenda. Were he to join the company, it must be under his terms and that meant rather more than tubes. 'To continue in the company wasn't really my future. The only way to survive [for him to survive] was to give some soul to the metal and

The working and shaping of steel tubing is still an in-house speciality. These skills – and the necessary tooling – might easily, and disastrously, have been lost in the rush to aluminium and carbon fibre mass production that has characterised the last two decades of bicycle manufacture.

Strength and precision are key to the process. Hand checking and finishing are taken very seriously on this production line.

the soul of cycling is the baseline of Columbus, to transform raw material into living material … cycling allows us to give passion, soul, culture."

The Latin word which gives us our aesthetic embraces a wide and nuanced definition but, at root, it means to perceive or know via the senses, all five senses. It develops, therefore, a more abstract purport, dealing with the critique which stems from perception, that branch of study we call aesthetics. This is what Colombo refers to. Even as we walk from the open concrete road into the gaping maw of the huge blockhouse of the factory and storage facility, the lines of bicycles with Cinelli frames standing like statues in the adyton of a temple, remind us of just this. The transformation of rough ore into gleaming artefact. Early blacksmiths were, according to the myth of Hephaestus, smith of the Olympian gods, ritually lamed so that they could not run away in order to hire out their unique and magical skills to the highest bidder. For they alone could take the lumps of glinting meteorite dug out of the earth and fashion of it swords, spear heads, braziers, cauldrons. (Hence the legend of Arthur tugging the sword from the stone, a mythic icon, or image, of the same idea.)

The shop floor, vast, cavernous as any subterranean goblins' hall, is much like any other – machines, dull greyness, wooden racks, greasy with use and age, home to lines of mandrels, dyes, formers. The machines are mostly quite elderly, of an earlier generation. Colombo explains that, when the companies were involved in the manufacture of mass-produced, cheap bikes, in the boom of the '70s and '80s, the work was done by automatic machines, robotic plant pumping out the bits and pieces as fast as they could go. Two million tubes per annum. The only handwork involved was the pressing of buttons, the flicking of switches. The advent of a crisis in steel production and the attendant slump in manufacturing, coupled with, even hastened by, a drop in demand for bicycles, nearly scuppered the company. Luckily, Colombo had insisted that they keep the old plant and now it is that older generation of machines which does the work, machines which depend on the feel, the hands, of those who operate them – here, a small force of seven or eight men.

Cold pilgering. Butting, shaping and profiling tubes to suit their end purpose.

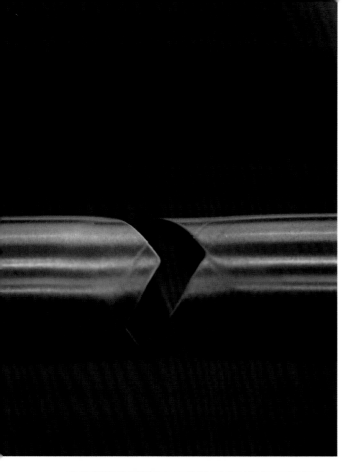

TOP LEFT
The results of a failure test.

ABOVE
Columbus measure the Ultimate Tensile Strength of their tubing before and after it has been worked.

TOP RIGHT
If it's not straight, then it's not much use.

LEFT
Antonio Colombo (left) talking shop with a colleague.

More intricate profiles require closer inspection.

39

The shaping of a pair of steel forks requires tapering. The old machine will perform the function capably but with one drawback: the stretching of the metal attenuates the thickness of the tube's wall. The crown of the fork retains the original diameter, the lower end is reduced. This may enjoin a comparable loss of strength. However, there is one newer machine in the factory which obviates this, using a technology which was, in fact, invented by two Germans, for heavy industrial purposes, in the late 19th century. The so-called cold pilgering process relies on four main actions: the tube containing a forming mandrel is pushed backwards and forwards through enclosing ring dies and, simultaneously, it rotates. It performs, therefore, a sort of to and fro shimmy, a jazzy sort of a dance, a syncopation which ensures that the metal retains the same thickness even as it is tapered, end to end. Cool. The process was adapted for the manufacture of vastly more slender tubing for bikes – and ski poles – in the 1940s. There were, once, twelve such machines in the Columbus works. To contemplate four tubes which illustrate the genesis of finely raked tapered tube from initial pipe shape is to indulge in a moment of aesthetic shiver.

The celebrated Laser, which married the artistic vision of Colombo and the engineering skill of the man who welded every Laser frame, Alessandro Pesenti, typifies the generating spirit and ethos of the Columbus-Cinelli enterprise: a fusion of design, art, technology, and restless inventive curiosity. Between 1981 and 1991 some 300 Laser frames were built, a third for professional riders. Hans-Henrik Oersted, of Denmark, set the sea-level Hour Record at Bassano del Grappa in the Trentino on a Laser in 1985, and in 1991, the Laser Evoluzione, a wonder of grace and fine craftsmanship, won the Compasso d'Oro, the highest accolade in the design world.

And the Laser is back, despite Pesenti's protests that he is too old (67); that it takes two months to build a single frame and that he doesn't want to spend the rest of his life welding frames. *'E allora, cosa face?'* Pesenti relents. Twenty-one, I'll build twenty-one. And so he did and so the idea did not go away because now they're going to be made of carbon (Pesenti supervising) … a limited output of around 250. Limited edition … the mark of the elite.

Columbus tubing has been used in products as diverse as office furniture, motorcycles and aircraft but it is in the construction of the bicycle that the name Columbus resonates most.

Whilst not quite unsung, the tubing of a bicycle often plays second fiddle to some of the more noticeable elements of the whole machine. However, innovation such as the unseen helical reinforcement within SLX tubing has a profound effect on the overall feel of the bike.

Handlebars and stems were the mainstay of company production, but small volumes of high quality steel road racing frames, most notably the Supercorsa, were also made.

"The key thing was that when you got to 13 or 14, suddenly you became aware of the bicycle, the actual bicycle, and the absolute key things to have were a Cinelli stem and bars."
Sir Paul Smith

CINELLI

A contemporary of both Gino Bartali and Gentullio Campagnolo, Cino Cinelli raced with some success as a professional cyclist, winning both the Tour of Lombardy and Milan san Remo in 1938 and 1943 respectively. It's arguable, though, that Cinelli made his biggest mark as an equipment producer when he hung up his professional wheels in 1946 and turned his attention to the bars, stems and frames that assured Cinelli a special place in the hearts of cyclists the world over.

Inside the Temple of Janus in ancient Rome stood a bronze statue of the god with two faces, looking both ways. His name, from *ianua*, 'a door', suggests way in and way out, beginnings. In starting any enterprise, the magic of Janus was needed because there is a lucky and an unlucky way of setting out. The fact that our word *sinister* is the Latin for 'left' is rooted in the classical notion that omens observed to the left – the flight of a numinous bird, for instance – were generally thought unpropitious. Janus's month began the year and, when Rome was at peace, the doors of his arch-like shrine were kept closed, locking in the turbulent spirit of war. Janus is used by some thinkers to represent the philosophical notion of emergence , that expression of the unity of separate components of a whole, (war/peace, open/shut) but also 'the synergystic effects produced by wholes that are the very cause of the evolution of complexity in nature'. All the bits adding up to a total greater than their sum. That, by and large, is to what Paul Smith alludes in the reverie of the teenage boy of his era, fired by the beauty of the Cinelli stem and bars which went to make the bicycle entire so special, so much more than the sum of its parts.

We are shown into Antonio Colombo's office in the new premises outside Milan to wait for him. We're early? He's delayed? Doesn't matter. I pick up a Cinelli catalogue. (Columbus took over Cinelli in 1978.) Everything with the singular name Cinelli on it – bars, stem,

Tradition and technology are well met with the Supercorsa. Italian craftsmen, often from the same family, build each frame ... with Columbus tubing, naturally.

ABOVE
The famous bottom bracket shell with the spoiler and built in cable guides, a classic Cinelli component which can be found on other makers bikes as well.

RIGHT
Meticulous attention to detail always.

frame, tape – comes from the Columbus operation now, but it is still Cinelli. Semper Cinelli, semper fidelis. I turn, idly, to a page advertising the famous (infamous) Spinaci handlebar extensions which were banned by the UCI after a particularly dangerous Tour de France course in 1997. But they were hailed by many as an innovation of insight, brilliance, a classic case of ingenuity coupled with simplicity of solution and design. The adjustable and comfortable Spinaci bar mimicked the position adopted by pro riders when they relaxed by leaning forward to put their forearms on the central part of the handlebars. Claudio Chiappucci was a convinced devotee. 'I put them on for all kinds of races…I felt I could control my bike so much better in decisive race situations as well as in moments of "relax" …' The ban caused great hurt at Columbus and, unrevoked, it still does. With Antonio Colombo being the sort of man he is (owner of a gallery of Contemporary Art in Milan), the hurt is expressed vividly in the catalogue. A small cartouche contains the famous line spoken by Aeneas to Dido at the opening of Book II of the Aeneid when she asks him to tell her and her court – their eyes and ears intent on him, in a penetrating silence – of the horrors of the Fall of Troy.

infandum regina iubes renovare dolorem.

O queen it is too horrible to speak of. To relive such grief.

Here, in the inner, light-filled cave of thinking, in what many must call a sanctuary of classic Italian design and technical excellence, as elite as you can get, a poignant ache of the modern day expressed in the Latin of one of Italy's finest poets twenty-one centuries before.

Let the man himself, Antonio Colombo, speak: 'Giving a name to a product is part of its design. That is why, for us, the term "accessory" is never under-rated. Of course it alludes to something secondary, superfluous, marginal, perhaps. But our goal is not to give you Parts and Accessories. We want to pass on some Cinelli chromosomes. Always … a concentrate of design, technology, competition and art.'

Sadly Cinelli no longer make their handlebars in Italy. Production has been moved 'offshore' and, although they do make bikes and frames in Italy, the much anticipated Laser project was still at the drawing board stage when we visited. Luckily we were able to see construction of the iconic Super Corsa which is still lovingly made in Italy, as it always has been, and can trace its lineage back more than 50 years. A dedicated workshop builds the lugged frames to order using Columbus tubing and a decidedly retro 1in headset. They are available as either a road or a track version but both feature the famous fastback stay design and the distinctive slotted 'spoiler' bottom bracket.

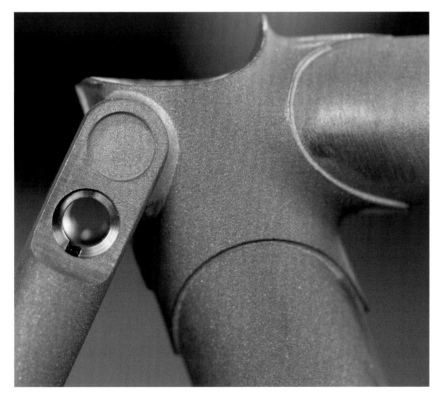

The signature seat cluster before and after.

FRAMES • Montreal, Canada

Guru work in titanium, steel and carbon. The workmanship is exceptional and the finish is immaculate whichever material is used. The Photon takes more than 40 hours to make.

GURU

As to the meaning of *guru*, opinions are divided, but the traditional explanation is that, in Sanskrit, *gu* stands for darkness and *ru* for the disperser of shadows, thus a teacher. Thus, the founder of Guru took the name 'based on the bicycle's capacity to teach life lessons and inspire'. Does that sound rarefied? I think it's meant to. Certainly much of what the Guru people say about themselves elevates the application of technology into a seriously cerebral experience, an almost higher mathematical abstraction. For we enter the world of morphology, of calculus, of near mystic union between bike and rider and road. Very well.

Let us consider those beautiful moments when, on a bike, we feel totally at one with the machine, rapt in a complete and complex harmony of movement, caught up in an ecstasy which is the sum of mind, body and mechanical efficiency, when the bike seems to run free as of its own accord, its own will, responding to a power generated by us in total symbiosis. In other words, more colloquially: you're on fire … riding out of your skin … in the zone … on song. Bliss.

Such perfection – not always in our immediate grasp – would seem to lie at the heart of what the Guru team offers: custom-built and hi-tech in concert to make a frame exactly suited to the rider. The pains they take to establish size and configuration of the frame are truly astonishing. Here are the bare bones of the process: extensive measurement of the rider, measurement data inputted into a proprietary algorithm* from which can be produced

* Algorithm (from algorismus, the Arabic system of numbers) may be defined as a set of rules that precisely defines a sequence of operations, so a collection of measurement data from which a conclusion may be drawn.

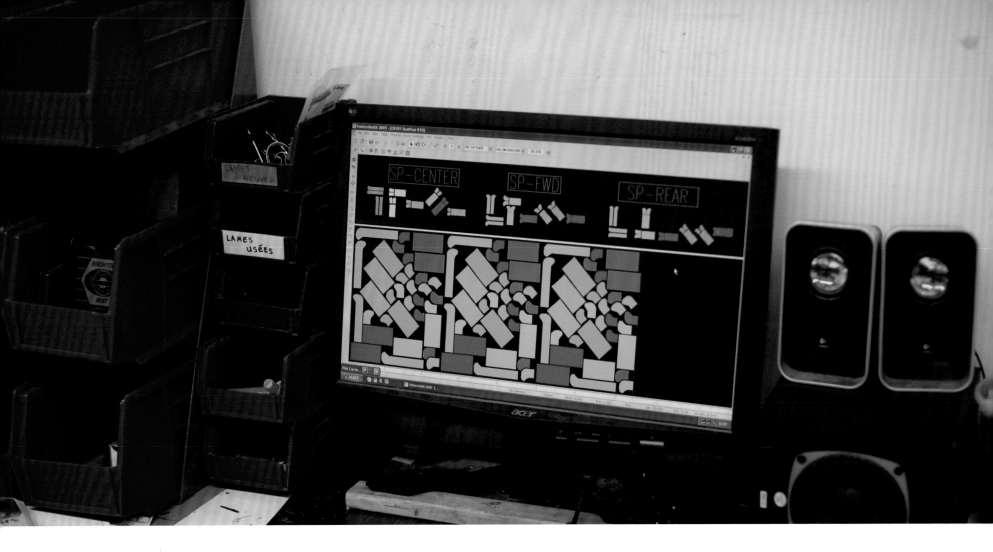

ABOVE
At the outset, carbon sheets are plotted and cut using computers. The material is expensive so that it's important to use as much of each batch as possible.

RIGHT
Carbon sheets are pre-impregnated with resin (known as prepeg). They are cut and laid out in such a way as to take advantage of the direction of the fibres in them: layering the sheets criss-cross allows the designer to tune the ride.

Individual carbon tubes are formed using a pressurised bladder-moulding technique over a mandrel before being baked and then joined together into a frame with carbon wrapping.

Exacting production values, carbon wrapping, vacuum moulds and high temperatures help to make the Guru Photon one of the lightest and stiffest bikes around. The same technologies are used throughout the range.

OPPOSITE PAGE
The son of a tailor, Toni Giannascoli (left), boss of Guru, is a keen engineer with a scientific mind. Combining science and tailoring to create bespoke bicycles was an obvious choice for him.

base geometry design – a Computer Aided Design [CAD] – which is sent back to the retailer for consultation with the customer. Any tweaks required? The CAD is returned to Guru and work can begin. The custom side of the job has been covered. Now for the technology, in titanium, carbon, steel or aluminium. But, more needs to be said about the intricacies of their assessment of a rider. It's based on the principle that the bike encapsulates 'the ultimate interface between man [man as human being] and road, one that should feel like a natural extension of your body… For us, custom-built is not an exercise in vanity or luxury – it's all about precision serving performance'. Guru are exceptional in that they also make custom-built carbon frames. This is a tricky thing to do; it's expensive and time-consuming. Some said that they didn't believe that Guru actually made the frames themselves, rather they were brought in from elsewhere and badged in Montreal. The truth is evident, however: the computerised drawings, the lay-up room with mandrels, blanks and blades, the limp and shapeless socks of impregnated fibres changed into more familiar light and stiff hollowed forms with heat and pressure. Stack-a boxes full of these odd yet costly pieces wait their turn to have glue applied and to mate with what is hoped will be their lifetime partner. The assembly is kept in a (sterile) vacuum before quality control. (They subject everything they make to Finite Element

Analysis, FEA, which means testing to destruction.) There's no cold setting with a carbon frame so the phrase 'heat of the moment' is pretty apt.

The history of custom building is intimately linked with road racing. Although many professionals rode what appeared to be team machines, in fact they preferred to go to a frame-builder whom they had used and trusted. Decals and enamel were no more than a simple disguise, a discretion to appease sponsors. Amateur riders and racers, even without wishing or hoping to become professional, always wanted a similar state-of-the-art frame, a bike that would serve them as well as the best. The growing popularity of custom-built frames exactly mirrors the increase in popularity of cycling per se. It is a fact that, if you ride a bike in America, it's because you have money. The high preponderance of professional people who cycle in the USA is an indicator of that. But this reflects what is becoming a general trend: the desire for the ultimate in a bike and the spending power to fund purchase of it, to ride a machine on a par with what the pros ride, even simply for pleasure … even the odd fun of gruelling long-distance sportives. Guru recognise and embrace this whole-heartedly. It promotes a confident argument for the advantage of custom building, even if they do (unnecessarily?) stress the need for performance, saying that a bike built to

Cutting slots by hand in an almost finished carbon frame requires a firm grip and nerves of steel. One slip and the job is ruined.

Every frame is sanded, inspected and polished before being handed over to the paint department.

OPPOSITE PAGE
Although they call it a factory rather than a work-shop, the Guru facility in Montreal is still very hands-on. Visual checks at each stage of the process are crucial.

the exacting criteria of the Guru design and manufacture will set up most cyclists in their 'sweet spot', responding to an optimum complement of power output, aerodynamics and weight distribution. A high-performance bike should be made to fit the individual, they insist, not the other way round. Rather charmingly, they call the perfect bike a cyclist's ideal soul mate. His or her other half. The other part that completes the perfect couple. To achieve that they need to examine in scrupulous detail a rider's morphology and story 'to unleash that individual's full potential'. Different body types ... they ask ... Different potential ... Different goals? The same bike? We don't think so.

This ought to be a truism. Clearly, they don't believe it is and apply a bewildering admix of maximal data and intelligence to fitting a bike to what they term:

1. The Century Rider, a rouleur type, whose bike design would be based on a classic geometry for all-round performance, slightly longer wheel base, and extended head tube to cushion a more upright position.

2. The Über Climber (German for Ace or Star), a slightly built rider with long femurs and a short torso who wants a stable, predictable bike that will fly downhill. Therefore, a relaxed seat angle, a lower bottom bracket, stretched out chainstays to spread the weight more evenly, plus a relaxed head angle and matching long rake.

3. The Crit[erium] Beast has short, strong legs and a larger upper body. They'd opt for a steep seat angle and short chainstays, a higher bottom bracket, steep head angle and short fork rake; all to allow for optimum handling and speed on corners.

This gives some notion of how finicky they are in paring design to use. 'It's not the easiest way to make a bike', they say, 'but it produces something special: a bicycle that is perfectly suited and absolutely balanced ... designed to make you go faster than you have ever gone before.'

One of the great things about being inspired by bike racing, the Tour de France in particular, is that any cyclist can ride the same roads, the same mountains as the pros. And, of course, to do that in any degree of comfort and to any level of satisfaction, they need a comparable bike. Guru make it their business to supply that bike. They even draw attention to the fact that they work in a 'cycling-crazy city [Montreal] that just happens to be a hotbed of aeronautical technology and expertise'. To the relevance of this conjunction, only a Guru owner can – and most assuredly will – attest.

CHAS ROBERTS

During the 19th century, as the gathering pace of the greater Industrial revolution increased the demand for an ever greater volume of production, manufacturing in both Britain and America, later in Germany, underwent a significant change. The workshop or domestic system, more cosily known as cottage industry, proliferated to supplement factory output. Craftsmen operating from their home were employed on a piecework basis. This could, in the hands of unscrupulous industrialists, be an extremely harsh practice. Outworkers were supplied with raw materials on receipt of a sometimes onerous deposit in cash, which, although they earned money for each item they produced, they struggled to pay off, against an ever-increasing burden of debt. Many different artefacts came out of this system – shoes, locks, watches, ready-made clothes, etc. – and, from 1854 onwards (the start of the Crimean War), large numbers of skilled outworkers in small workshops around parts of Birmingham and London were contracted to manufacture small arms for the British army, heavily engaged as it was in imperial duties of conquest and defence. In 1861, a number of small traders in Birmingham grouped together to found the Birmingham Small Arms [BSA] trade association which, as the demand for weapons declined, switched, in 1880, to the manufacture of bicycles. Thus, out of small workshops, were swords beaten into ploughshares. And, for reasons wonderful to relate if not to comprehend, the passion for the small workshop persisted, even to what became the classic reduction of cottage industry to kitchen table and back room, as in 'back-room boys' as certain inventors and theoretical technicians of the Second World War were known.

Chas Roberts: the man himself.

Winston checking the fork blades against each other.

Winston fine tuning a pair of fork blades prior to fitting into the crown.

Adrian cutting a bottom bracket thread.

Lining the blades up with the crown for final fitting.

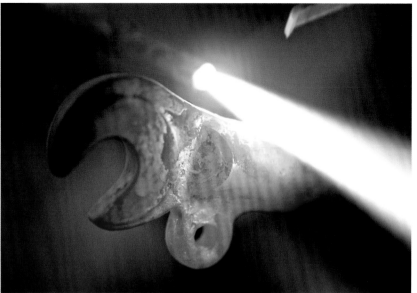

Winston is finally happy with the dry fit and lights up the brazing torch.

It was in the cellar of the family house in Sydenham, south London, that Charlie, Chas's father, worked on the first Roberts' frames. Charlie had built frames for other makers whose names resonate in the history of hand-building – Claude Butler, Freddie Grubb, Holdsworth – and branched out on his own in the 1960s. I first visited Chas (his father died a while back) at the present workshop in Croydon, just past The Drum and Monkey pub on Gloucester Road, cycling there on my then best bike, with a hand-built Alan Shorter frame. Wheeling it into the works, past the lustrous, sleek Roberts machines was what it must be like to tug a flea-bitten mongrel into the ring at Crufts. The technical assistant who greeted me looked at me and said, with no more than a twinkle of smile: 'How long have you had that saddle?' But then he told me of a man who, taking possession of his new Roberts, added the favourite, comfortable Brooks saddle he'd ridden for many years. This, in a curious way, encapsulates the Roberts philosophy: to fit the customer exactly, in every detail of manufacture.

I asked Chas whether his father had pushed his son to join him. 'No, not really. I was always stripping bikes down – get a Phillips, rebuild it as a dirt-track iron with cow-horn bars and knobbly tyres, just to be a bit flash. When most kids my age were doing a paper round, I was earning pocket money, helping Dad every night, brazing up carriers for Butler.' It was his initiation into the mystery of fusion of metals by heat and solder. And, the beginning of a father-son continuum. The fact that Chas designs every single Roberts himself, even if he can't get into the workshop as often as he likes – the business has to be managed, paperwork, bank manager, orders – means that every Roberts bike has what he calls 'a human face'. Mass-produced models speak *machine-made*. Even the top-end pro-style classy items 'as *ridden* by' are, as he puts it 'very aero-space but they have little character. We [he and his father] were always drawn by a bike, a frame, and that's the feeling that lasts'.

Chas is careful to find out what each customer, individually, wants from the bike and then takes the basic measurements which enable him to make the frame bespoke.* Weight, for instance, is important because a beanpole and a thickset individual may, in fact, have the same skeleton. Roberts is particularly concerned about tailoring a bike for a woman and a lot of women do come to him for his bikes. He explains: 'Acquiring a properly-sized woman's bicycle has tended to be a matter of luck. In most bike shops, the choice for women is limited. It's not long since the industry standard idea of

*The word, 'bespoke' in written record only since 1865, is much overused these days, of cakes to apartments, but it ought to denote a single item made by one craftsman or craftswoman, for an individual customer to whom she or he has spoken direct.

TOP LEFT
Pre-finishing joints with a belt sander before the emery paper and elbow grease take over.

ABOVE
The bikes that emerge from south London metal artist Chas Roberts' shop, have graced the track, the road and the open country. People travel long distances to order a Roberts' bike and once they've got one they usually travel some more. We've seen Roberts' bikes in the middle of the Gobi Desert en route to ... somewhere or other.

LEFT
Adrian at the checking table: steel frames sometimes need teasing back into alignment once they've been heated.

a lady's bike was a gent's bike with a low-slung top tube to allow skirts to be worn, topped off with a wide, sprung saddle. Most women had to make do with the smallest man's frame they could find, combined with ever-shorter handlebar stems and saddles pushed as far forward as the rails allow.' Worse still was having to use a male partner's wrongly-sized hand-me-down cycle components. Effectively, a woman had to put up with an awkwardly sized machine, just as children have, until now, had to start on Lilliputian versions of the adult machine.

In contrast with this apparently solemn summation of the Roberts ethos, let's counter with the evolution of his prototype MTB, with its trademark unique horseshoe rear seat stays. 'We made that when the MTB fraternity was just getting going [c.1982] and we didn't know what to call it. We had a graduate working for us, a fan of *Viz* magazine. Every other sentence seemed to have the dog's bollocks in it. So, that's what we called our mountain bike – D.O.G.S. B.L.X.'

He has his detractors, the surly old-school cynics who say, for instance, that the ultra-chic *Rapha* is giving cycling a bad name (by candid enthusiasm, presumably) and grumble that Roberts overcharges, so much extra for bloody this and bloody that, all overpriced and overblown. There's no accounting for ignorance. It's a sour British flaw, attuned to the cloth-cap image of the bike, deprecating what is top drawer, calling it pretentious. How we cleave to failure. But, things are changing. As cycling gets more expensive, it's an indication that the image is more classy, more desirable. Roberts is agreeably unselfconscious about the superb quality and design of his bikes but it cannot mask the passion, the thought, the constant substratum of inventive energy behind the sketch he pulls out of a drawer, a scrap of paper cut to shape, a new musing on disc brakes. This is what he calls 'playing around the edges'. From this come the advances, the special

touch. It's part of the responsibility he feels, the pride in making something with his name on it, realising the promise of excellence and precision.

A Roberts fitting is very similar to that of a tailor fitting for a suit – I have experienced both. The calculation of size, by tape and the trained eye and expertise of the tailor (from the French *tailleur,* a cutter). The word we know as meaning dimension or measure, comes from assize, (from the French *asseoir,* 'to sit') for a regular sitting of assessors to fix taxes, laws, measurements ... And so, in a long discussion, Roberts asks what I want the bike for, am I dedicated more to speed or comfort, how far I intend to ride it. Whether I want British or continental positioning for the back brake lever. Hm? Left-hand drive means the left hand on the bars while right-hand indicates right, and vice versa. Aha. He indicates various points in some of the bikes in the front room of the shop, to show how each machine is adapted to specific purpose. All this before I step over to the measuring jig – for height and inside leg (a bar adjusted to the crutch as it were a saddle). Lengths of upper body, femur joint to knee as the leg rotates, width of shoulders (a broken collarbone can cause one shoulder to tilt lower than the other), arms ... shoe size ...weight ...

Before the exploratory interview and sizing, which together last an hour, Roberts hands me the form on which he'll copy all the measurement details. I enter name, address and so on and sign it at the bottom.

'You don't need to do that yet', he says.
'It's okay, I trust you.'
'Your first mistake', he says.
'What's that?'
He smiles. 'To trust me.'
Very south London, that.

The garage sale aspect common to the back rooms of many small builders is reassuring: it means they've been doing it a long time.

From the initial bundle of pipes to the fully painted,
finished product, the Rourke operation is small but
totally self-contained.

ROURKE

We walk out of the rain into the triple garage which houses the Rourke workshop in a secret
location. You remember Ralph Waldo Emerson's dictum about people beating a path to the
door of the man who has invented a world-beating mousetrap? That's exactly what Jason
Rourke does not want. 'Imagine, my whole day would be taken up with mitherers.' I first heard
the word years past in Lincolnshire. It means to be bothersome, tedious … so, Rourke *fils*
and I swept into a lively conversation about dialect before getting onto the main business: the
Rourke frame.

'We're about the shape of the bike', he says. 'I'd recognise one of ours in silhouette.' Cue the
unique feature of the Rourke frame, about which they are jealously protective: the wrap-over
clenching of the back stays round the junction of top and seat tubes. Jason has been asked
how it's done, has overheard people guessing how it's done (all wrong) and, even as we
watched him fashioning the piece, we felt the slight, furtive mischief of it – a secret into which
we were initiated and to which we must cleave in silence.

Where, then, do the clients get measured, if not here? In the shop, in Stoke-on-Trent,
founded by Rourke *père*, former champion bike racer. 'Was it your father who taught you
frame-building?' 'No, he never made frames; he just rode, designed and sold them.' He
points to a child's bike, 24" wheels, at the side of the workshop – 'that's the bike that made
me a frame builder, when I was 11.' (Another even smaller machine stands in the far corner,
his first bike, with his Dad's name on the down tube.) The pink'un was originally burgundy,
Saronni, red, but when they loaned it to a friend's daughter, they repainted it. Riding a bike

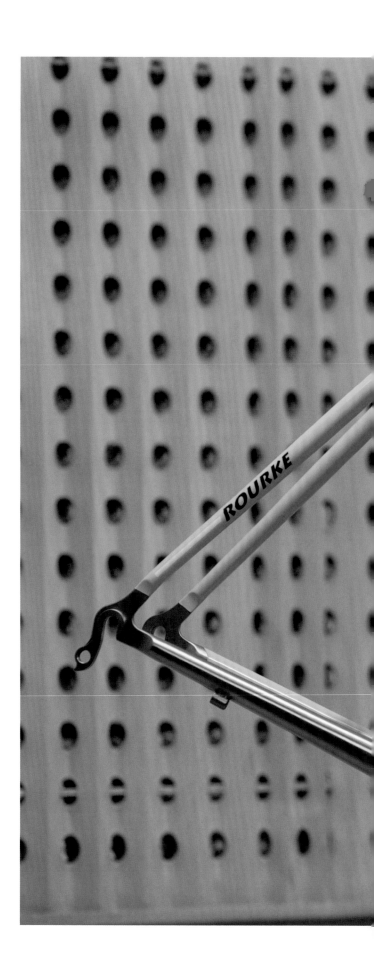

Tig welding and fillet brazing combine to deliver the cleanest look, the strongest joint and the greatest variety of geometry. Certain tubes, oval in section, for example, don't lend themselves to a lug, so an alternative approach is needed.

designed by his father was cool, but it was a combination of the feel of the larger machine and the growing awareness that something magical had gone into the making of it which seeded his ambition. The wrap-over stays were invented some forty years back by father and the then frame-builder, Roger Kowalski. It was a 'strength and aesthetic thing'. The next frame builder, Paul Washington, taught Jason. He'd been a glass-blower, and the student is full of praise for his tutor's brazing technique. 'The man's control was phenomenal, he could run brass up a bank' ie uphill, in deftly coaxing the flow of the brass along the seam by the subtle play of the torch's flame.

The bike fitting is done in the upstairs club-room, Kelly's [as in Sean] Bar, of the shop. There's a white-frame bike standing by the bar, the man's name painted on it. 'We fit by sitting the customer on a bike, we get their shape and balance by looking at them. Jigs? No. You can't measure bones.' They've had twins come in – you'd suppose that they'd be the same, wouldn't you? No. Quite different. If this smacks of the arcane, then it stems from Rourke senior's approach to the bicycle: that all the know-all jabber about this or that machine, slavering over the lovely class of this, the superior nature of that, gloating upon shiny components, the *apparatus criticus* of

bike-pornography, is nonsense. It's the engine on the machine which counts and the philosophy (so to aggrandise a bit of homespun truth) which follows the Rourke bike out of the shop onto the road comes from the man who was national champion seven times: 'Just get on the bike and ride it till you can't breathe, ride your pan out.'

They get orders from all over – we noted Singapore, Bristol, Cumbria, Knutsford, Paris, York, America … and they tend to encourage buyers to come to the shop for the fitting, albeit they can work from the more conventional specification, and they will always change a frame if they're asked. They also restore – a Colnago waits upstairs in the paint room for the top coat. This is now Ernie's domain, a friend of Jason since they were both thirteen, drawn together by fishing and they still fish. Ernie quit a building job to come to work with his old mucker and he shows me the new quick-drying lacquer, the cabinet of pots containing all the hues he needs to make pretty well any colour in the spectrum. A read-out of the precise recipe of mixes, a measuring scale will produce the right shade in any quantity. He paints the frames always in the same sequence, tube by tube, turning the frame over in a rhythmic flow which makes for even surfacing and speed of work.

ABOVE AND RIGHT
Jason was given a made-to-measure bike for his twelfth birthday – undoubtedly a key experience in his frame-building career. After leaving school, he went to work with Paul Washington, a one-time glass blower turned frame builder – an exceptional adept in the control of heat and solder.

Jason spends a lot of time at the jig to make the mitres accurate, and then assembles the tubes dry before any heat is applied. The joints must sit together perfectly both before and after brazing.

The 'famous' fork bending block.

The seat stay/seat tube 'wrap' is a Rourke signature detail.

Downstairs again, I investigate an unlovely curved wedge of ancient softwood anchored to a bench by an iron shackle. Along the centre of the block, end to end, runs a semicircular groove. This is the form for every set of forks that leaves the place, of classic rake. Italian, I'd call it, gracious and handsome, imparting comfort and exceptional bike-handling balance, particularly on descents. 'We're a bit hot on the look of our forks', says Jason, as I admire a veritable item of workshop history. They do fit carbon forks, yes, and Jason expatiates on a puzzle. 'A set of forks made out of 753 is about as uncomfortable as you can get – you can't relax on the hoods – yet you can have dead straight forks which are wonderfully kind to ride. How can that be?' He adds a coda – traditionalist as his father manifestly is, he doesn't mind carbon … 'it's aluminium he hates'.

I ask if he ever signs a frame. Yes, if he's asked. For a while, there was an artist working in the shop next door, in town, and he used to paint customers' names on the top tube, by hand. A signature to mark out the frame but, then, there is a signature in all these frames, the four or five which get made here each week. For, despite the presence of angle-grinders, small electric belt polishers, the handwork is central: the filing, the cutting with hacksaw, the setting of tubes by eye, the marking with a black felt-tip, the squinting at location, the clamping in position and the tig welding. It's a sort of prestidigitation … magical sleight of hand.

ABOVE
As a patriotic English builder, Rourke prefers to use Reynolds tubing but he will also happily use whatever is best adapted to the individual needs of a client.

LEFT
Cutting a head tube.

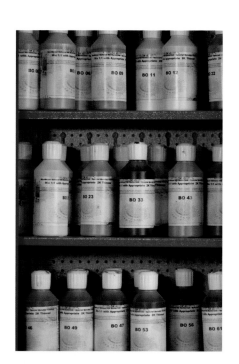

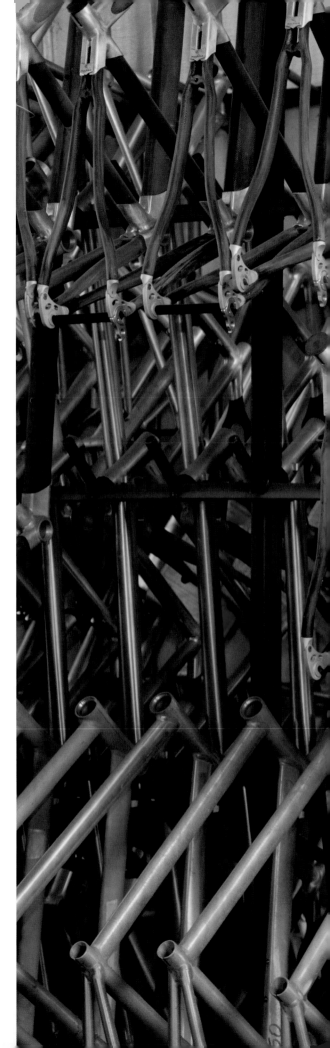

FRAMES • La Fuye, Hommes, France

CYFAC

The French place high premium on the quality of *terroir*, the infusion of the earth's quality into what comes out of the earth – different soils add variety of taste to vintages, breeds of cattle and sheep and the cheeses that emanate from their milk … and so on. CYFAC [pron. see-fack], *Cycles Fabrication Artisanale de Cadres* – craft-made bicycle frames – vaunts its own roots among the vineyards of the Loire valley and in the heart of the tranquil, bike-friendly country lanes of Touraine near its factory in La Fuye. If this seems fanciful, then you are not paying attention. For their attention is to detail and the slogan 'made by hand in Fuye' is no idle boast.

CYFAC's founder, Francis Quillon, began as a frame builder and was of the precise measurement school: a bike had to fit its rider like a bespoke suit; it had to be comfortable over long distances; it had to be of extreme high quality, in material and manufacture. This ethos translates into what may be taken as the CYFAC watchword 'posture'. Horse-riders speak of having a good seat, a CYFAC bike promises just that. The concept is hardly revolutionary – Italian stage-racing bikes of the '40s and '50s had a longer wheel base and steeper fork rake than most in order to accommodate stressful hours riding over mountainous landscape. The CYFAC Postural System is the direct result of some twenty years of research and analysis at the Centre of Sports Medicine in Lyon.

Quillon, himself a former national amateur sprinter, who'd learnt his craft on the hoof – mending his team-mates machines, applying a native inquisitiveness to the machine's structure – began to make frames in his garage in 1982. Hand-built by one man, customised to sponsors' requirements and the painting of the frame is still a signal part of the CYFAC operation, extending minute attention to detail of construction to the look, and glossy feel, of the skeleton around

France, for so long home to bicycle culture, has surprisingly few bicycle manufacturers. Cyfac machines, however, whether in carbon, steel or aluminium, are world class.

RIGHT
Cyfac's carbon Absolu, is the flagship model of this medium-volume French producer.

LEFT
The production line.

LEFT
Two different carbon sheets.

BELOW
The hair thickness Kevlar strands.

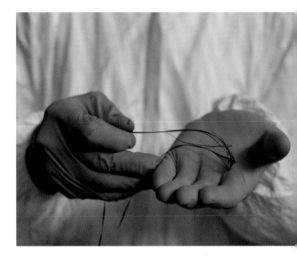

ABOVE
Cutting and facing a bottom bracket shell.

LEFT
The layup process is crucial to the way a carbon fibre bicycle behaves. The quantity, direction and type of the fibres and the amount of resin added to the matrix all have their part to play in dealing with pedalling forces and road conditions. Making a very stiff bike is easy but making a stiff bike that is also comfortable to ride is rather more tricky.

which a bike, whether for touring or professional specification, is formed. They have a palette of some 30,000 colours and shades to choose from, so the matter of bespoke is about as refined as it can get. This scrupulous concentration on detail isn't just a catchphrase, either: it is, they say, the leitmotif of all the work that goes on in the CYFAC plant. They order tubing direct from Columbus of Padua, and exercise firm control of quality, profile, size. They cover every aspect of the frame size, 'from A to Z', vis à vis the rider for whom it is intended, accepting that if there is something wrong with the result, then it is their fault. And we observe it, close hand.

The welder retreats inside his booth, pulls down the visor on his helmet and plays his torch on the metal. Through my own visor, that makes everything dark, I watch the dart of the gas jet, quivering like a glow-worm eager for some action in the grass verge. When the welds are done, our man takes the frame across to a work bench, fixes it in the jaws of a vice and begins the five-hour process of filing down the surplus of the metallic scab at the joint. Intermittently, he smears pig fat to soften it and then rubs it down with

glass paper. I ask if he gets the lard from the butcher. A laugh. 'Used to, but now it's manufactured.' On the frame, for the time being an anonymous bracket of dull metal, is written in marker pen the name of the client for whom it is destined, and thus it becomes special, singled out. But that individuation is recorded, too, on the manifest of the order: all details of angle, slope, length, diameter … Their 80 dealerships worldwide can measure direct from the central web data bank.

Hanging on the wall, near the paint shop, a further example of singularity: the frame for an American catalogue, gaudily decorated with images representative of France (you know how they just love the old world over in the new): Marianne … Mont Saint-Michel … bunch of grapes … Eiffel Tower … and, for reasons unexplained, François Rabelais, a racy choice of Gallic icon.

Quillon is still involved with the company, as honorary President, and he still rides a bike, but he stepped aside from the manufacturing arm when carbon came in. He realised that this new material required a technical expertise

with which he was not familiar; equally that it was going to revolutionise the making of frames. It was 2002, he was nearly 60, CYFAC as it existed was too dependent on him. Loyalty to the company he founded yielded to the vital need for change, development, to preserve the identity and the integrity of the company, based on the core idea of customising. CYFAC, therefore, adapted, and, after first using carbon lugs, two years ago switched to wrapping for the joints. (Of the 600 frames they make annually, 50 per cent are carbon, 25 per cent each aluminium or steel.) Layers of Kevlar are applied and glued; the Kevlar, when teased apart, a knit of fibres fine as spider's silk.

I walk past a vast bit of antique massively engineered tooling plant, made in Russia, 1964, to read a number of documents pinned to one wall, bruiting success in professional racing, attesting customer satisfaction – not always without reservation: one individual, unused to such a carefully tailored machine, finding the bike too skittish, not immediately comfortable, in need of adjustment – and recounting the history of the company in the last decade. Reference is made to a 'Kafkaesque battle with the French

economic administration' to save it and I proceed to the office to ask the Director, Aymeric le Brun, to explain, please. He beckons me into the board room. It's evidently a sensitive subject. Although he speaks good English, the story comes in French.

CYFAC was sold in 2002. In brief, the parent company was declared bankrupt in 2007 and, without funds, its CEO, a bon viveur businessman wholesaler, more interested in golf and cigars than bicycles, was fired by the shareholders to be replaced by a banker. However, the smaller partner CYFAC had money and, because of fiscal law, could not, therefore, go to a tribunal to extricate itself and be quit of the liabilities incumbent on its owner. The legal entanglement took some seven months to unpick and to allow CYFAC to move forward, once more independent.

One final question I put to le Brun. 'Francis Quillon was, in essence an engineer, I suppose you'd say?'
    He smiles. 'No, he's a genius.'

Painting and finishing is something that CYFAC takes very seriously. Done wholly in-house, often incorporating many personal and intricate designs to order of the customer, the finished products are handsome, indeed.

ALEX SINGER

Alex Singer [pron. san-jaire] born in 1905, left his native Hungary for Paris in 1923. A passionate cyclotouriste, he worked as a joiner, then did a stint with a pharmacist, before learning his trade with an Italian bike-maker and setting up on his own as a builder of specialist bikes in 1938. He and his wife rented a shabby premises at number 53 rue Victor Hugo, in the north-west Paris suburb of Levallois-Perret, not far from a stadium named after the triple Tour de France winner, Louison Bobet. They lived over the sales room and workshop. The shop-front has been modernised – just – but the place has hardly changed.

Conscripted into the French army in 1939, Singer was captured at Dunkerque, spent two days in captivity, escaped and made his way back to Paris and lived under cover for the rest of the war, building the specialist bikes on the pattern of the lightweight steel machine -frame, components and lights, all refined and reduced in weight through the ingenious and innovative design which became his trademark. The Grand Prix Duralumin, a rough riding extended technical contest for bikes robust enough to withstand hilly and rugged roads, had been initiated in 1935. Singer entered four tandems in 1939 – a four-stage ride over 553km held in the Vosges mountains. He brought the lightest machine to the event, at 13kg, one kilogram less than the previous winner. In 1946, at Colmar, Alsace, three of his bicycles won first prize: the tandem, Cyclo-camping category and the Prototype, with a machine weighing 6.875kg (minus tyres). Singer competed in the 1949 Paris-Brest-Paris on a bike fitted with a 28-spoke front wheel and a rear wheel which had 18 spokes on the freewheel side, only 9 on the other side. That wheel covered 5000km without going out of true.

In this carbon era, such a weight is not untoward, but for a steel machine then? And the Singer enterprise strives, still, to reduplicate the archetypal model pioneered by Alex. After the war, materials were scarce, the advent of a wider manufacture of cheaper cars triggered a serious decline in the popularity of the bicycle and Alex, now joined by his two nephews, Ernest (who assembled the bikes and made components) and Roland Csuka (who built the frames) working long hours, six days a week, kept the business going. Even so, Roland worked in a car factory during the week to subvent the bicycle business. But, the very dearth of materials prompted that most precious of resources in a man of ingenuity: the power to adapt. They couldn't get components, so they made their own and, when pressed to

say who had originally come up with the idea for a new part, the answer was always 'we all did, combined effort'.

At the heart of the Singer reputation was invention: the characteristic lug filed from welded X-section steel tubing; the slender, copper-chromed lightweight handlebar stem and pillar; the seat post cut across on a diagonal and held by an internal pin and bolt, obviating the need for a seat pin; the rod derailleur brazed onto the back of the seat tube; the cantilever brakes with blocks which tighten straight onto the rim, worked by double cables which reduce the pressure needed to apply the brake. The luggage carriers, back and front (to accommodate specialist leather luggage made by Gilles

Berthoud), are another trademark styling of the Singer bike. And the Singer name, particular as it is, has a unique identification: on a button on top of the stem is engraved the name and address of the owner. Among the many bikes hanging from a rail in the old workshop – I mean *old* … nothing has changed since Alex himself was working here – is the founder's own machine, dark blue frame, fabric chain-guard, swept bars for town use, and the address, 53 … Bicycle number 14 passed from Maria Singer to Roland (aged 14) and eventually to Olivier, Ernest's son, who now runs the business. If Alex founded the Singer bicycle enterprise, Ernest may be said to have brought it through financial crisis in the 65 years of his involvement in the company. Above his old work bench are pinned the specifications of all bikes which leave the premises. The heaps of old tyres, like giant worm casts, the discarded lengths of redundant tube, stems, bars, the pin-board racks of tools, the pigeon holes for bits and pieces – most, it must be said, which look either beyond use or usefulness but kept, as a sort of guarantee of the continuum which is practised here, the antique style, retaining *baraka*, the virtue in cherished objects, handled over years by a succession of Singer artisans. In accord with that, the same accoutrements of the work, the plying of ancient file to welds and brazes, the painting of orange Gomme-lacque from an old sardine tin onto cotton Tressostar tape to give the varnish a finish resistant to sweat and rain. Above the old lathe by one wall, a notice reminds the operator to replace the cover to ward off drips of rain (and consequent rust) from the leaky, tired old grimy glass roof overhead.

Pour faire ce métier, il faut être cycliste. To do this job you have to be a cyclist and Olivier, born in 1964, a cyclist since he was nine, races and rides as have they all, using the original bikes, to imbibe the spirit, maybe. 'Yes, we make fine bikes', he says, 'but for us, the most important consideration is the riding of them.' I ask him for whom they make frames and build bikes. 'We have three sorts of customer: one has lots of bikes and is very exacting in the specification of what he, or she, is after; second, someone just starting out who needs advice on what best to look for, based on where and how they want to ride, where they live, how old they are and so on; and third, the geek who comes in here with his head full of ideas he's got from books and the web and wants the all singing and dancing machine. So, we listen, and quietly guide him to what makes sense.'

That guidance is more of an instinct, a feel, than a precise analysis and Olivier is scathing about the school of thought which advocates minuscule measurements for the fitting of a bike to a client. Not necessary, he insists. That

OPPOSITE PAGE
Olivier Csuka has raced bicycles, restored bicycles and built bicycles. His passion is for a well-made bike suited, variously, to competition, shopping expeditions, about town rides …

ABOVE
The whole place is a veritable time warp, a sanctum dedicated to the Singer mystique.

Olivier modifying a seatpin.

An early brake system devised by Singer; part V brake, part cantilever.

Sealing cotton bar tape with a cellulose based fluid.

A very desirable top cap for a very elegant stem.

said, they are not inflexible. They accommodate an individual's ideas if they can, always on the proviso that what leaves number 53 is identifiably a Singer bike.

Handsome, sleek, unmistakeably classic in design, the Singer bikes which line the tiny showroom, near the counter on which stands an old lever-operated cash register, have a touch of antique class which even toe clips cannot efface. And the tradition.

In 2007, Ernest rode the Col de la Madeleine in the Alps, on his beloved

Singer bike, of course, at the age of 79. The last job he did in the workshop was to fill an order for a reproduction of the bike he'd built for the 1946 Concours Duralumin. Olivier, now faced with having to take over entirely, asked his father, 'But how will I make them?' Ernest said, 'You'll figure it out.'

His spirit is evidently here, a real presence in the place, and Olivier exudes it. 'I do not know what the future will bring', he says, 'but I know that it is not something which one watches from the sidelines. It has to be built, like the bicycles.'

Elegant chaos. The Singer establishment is part workshop, part warehouse, part museum of old frames, part sale-room. Bikes and bike components cluttered about the place, plus the tools and other paraphernalia needed to assemble them.

FRAMES • Padova, Italy

This is one of Massimo's personal projects: a gentleman's tourer par excellence.

FAGGIN

There is a hill in Udine, built, so legend has it, by the soldiers of Attila the Hun who needed a vantage point in the otherwise flat terrain. His men dug up soil and carried it in their helmets and upturned shields until ol' Attila was happy with his gazebo. I know of a hill built in similar, though peaceable, circumstances, so the legend may hold water. However, Udine later boasted a *velodromo* as well as its artificial prominence, and on this track Marcello Faggin of Padova, born in 1913, a natural racer who loved track racing above all, laid down a challenge to the professional rider Silvano Petrei. And beat him. That was not the apogee of his racing exploits – he and a friend were wont to ride events all over north-east Italy, cycling to and from the races – but it is proudly singled out as proof, if any were needed, of his talent in the saddle. He retired in 1932 and, in 1945, began the second phase of his life's work: the construction of bicycle frames.

His singular expertise in track riding made the frames he built in the tiny workshop in a suburb of Padova especially sought after and his intimate connexion with the local professional team Torpado (Torresini Padova) helped cement his reputation. As we heard at Selle Italia, this region of Italy has always been a hotbed of racing cycling. The very fact that two of the great monuments of professional cycling open and close the calendar – Milan-SanRemo, *La Primavera* (Springtime), and Giro di Lombardia, *La classica delle foglie morte* (Classic of the Dead Leaves) – hereabouts confirms that. Is there something in the fact that the area was known in classical times for its exceptional breed of racing horses, peerless steeds for the chariot race on the oval piste of the Circus Maximus in Rome?

Like many retired racers, Marcello could not shake off the bug and worked on as a manager and mechanic for the men of a younger generation. His frames, his wisdom trackside, his very presence, a stocky, balding man of steady gaze and easy poise ...

RIGHT
Maria Cristina, Marcello Faggin's daughter, continues the tradition, and prestige, of the Faggin name

ABOVE
Translating the data and measurements from plans and notes to the three dimension of the tubing on the jig constitutes the pivotal skill of frame building.

Massimo, the one-time apprentice, is now the master craftsman. He and his wife work together in the workshop every day.

Faggin bikes are highly reputed. Not offered to, or seeking, a mass market as some other makers, the Faggin machine has a well-established international customer base.

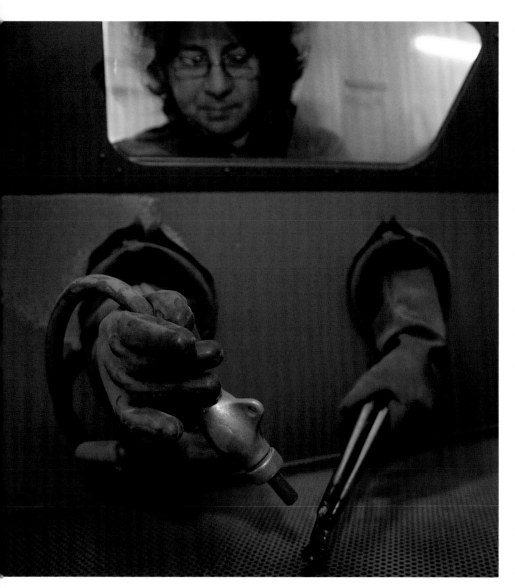

Sizing, cutting, brazing and sand blasting are all done in the same workshop. It is a one-stop shop for all things steel although carbon can be incorporated into some frames on request.

'He was a big-hearted man, generous, very warm.' So the youngest of his four daughters, Maria Cristina, tells me just after we arrive in the penumbral machine room of the original premises where the frames are still crafted. She is married to Massimo Francescon, who began as an apprentice to Marcello in 1976 when he was but 13 years old, and, together, they continue the tradition, the name, the class of the Faggin frame. Yes, she puts on the goggles and takes up (as well as carries) the torch, too. It's still a family affair. Indeed, all four daughters were helping their father as soon as they reached the age of fifteen, perfecting the skills of brazing and welding. In the 1970s they officially became members of the firm, contributing ideas to improvement of the antique excellence.

For a small operation such as that of Faggin, the links with successful riders is of paramount importance. It pays for publicity which a firm with limited finances cannot readily afford and the list of winners on Faggin frames is vast and egregious. A single postcard signed 'Alla ditta Faggin con simpatia, Eddy Merckx' ('To the Faggin house with affection, E.M.') says much, even if Massimo didn't work with Merckx until after the great Belgian's retirement. Class will always out. And it was with German teams that, pre-eminently, Faggin had success. The first Faggin world title – on the track in 1983 – added the precious rainbow colours to the company's logo. A year later, Roger de Vlaeminck, who had combined a dazzling career on both road and mud, asked the Faggin works to make cyclo-cross frames for his team and the Faggin frames have been ridden to victory by a number of Belgian cyclo-cross men since then.

The recent upsurge in demand for fixed machines among young fans has revived the Faggin fortune. A generation brought up on large profile, homogeneous aluminium, titanium and carbon has woken to the unique quality of a lissom steel frame, an uncluttered transmission which shows off the lines of the wheels and enhances the grace of the frame itself. These delicate characteristics point up the appeal of the Faggin trademark: beautiful shaping of a machine made for speed and touch handling. Just to walk by the samples on display in the rooms above the workshop at the Via Filiasi is to sink into a reverie at their sheer beauty of form.

One of these objects of wonder, the Cromovelato, exhibits a lustrous manner of finish: to a polished and enamelled chrome frame is added a coat of clear, coloured paint which shows off to brilliant effect the high gloss of the metal. Like the surface of a perfect intaglio.

Before we leave, we sit at the kitchen table and drink coffee which, miraculously, does not deliver a shocking jolt of adrenalin to the system, and regale ourselves on Cristina's home-made apple cake. And, secretly, I drool at the thought of the track bike I have just seen, the Faggin, on my way in.

Hand finishing is something that
Massimo relishes.

ABOVE
Refining the lugs with a tool resembling a dental
pick guarantees a flawless finish.

LEFT
Cleaning, trimming and reaming the head and seat
tubes ensures a precision fit for headsets and
seat pins.

The little workshop is an unassuming time capsule of artisanal excellence. The Faggin name draws many an admirer to the address in the suburbs of Padova.

The famous window with its birds was a feature of the workshop when Dario moved into the premises. Now that he's moved premises, will he adorn a window in the new place with them?

PEGORETTI

On the wall above the entrance to the paintshop in the premises – soon to be vacated – of the Pegoretti works, hangs a large sheet of paper, scrawled with signatures round the central motif: a caricature of the man Dario, sitting on an upturned tin tub, toasting a crab, skewered to the end of a pair of dislocated forks, over a small fire. The original poster was painted for a bike show in 2007 when Pegoretti was undergoing chemotherapy for cancer. (He is in remission.) Cancer is Latin for crab. It's almost a trademark with him, the jocularity, the word-play, the studied allusion.

He emerges from the office – too much time he has to spend in there, *ahimè*, three hours a day, more, hunched over a computer he complains, fielding enquiries, answering e-mails, this, that and the other distracting call on his energies. It's doubly hard because most of the messages are in English, although he speaks the language more than serviceably. But he leaves the cell of perdition and his body relaxes. We shake hands. He smiles, gestures round the workshop. The place is a mess, they're packing up for the move. One of his men, Diego, i/c paintshop, is breaking up redundant display stands, separating the metal bits from the wood – recycling. We go into the kitchen and Dario hands over a small plastic cup of the potent coffee which seems to fuel the Italians to some indefinable spurt of activity, mental or psychological, but clips my resistance to orderly thought processes with disturbing efficacy.

He started frame-building in Verona in 1975. No, it wasn't out of passion, a dream, an inner drive. It was money. He was racing with a small team which he also managed; there was no cash in that. 'I needed to make some money, so that meant a job.' It was his great luck that the man who employed him, Luigino Milani, became a central influence. After six months

91

working with Milani he was hooked. 'He taught me not only about making frames, but about how to live. He was a good man, a good teacher, a good father.' (He married Milani's daughter.) And, when Luigino died in 1990, Dario took over the business and opened his own shop the following year.

Aside from the incessant traffic on the internet, there are the visitors – around 300 to 400 every year, some who make an appointment to get measured for a frame, others just to stop by and take a coffee. He discusses the eventual bike with every client, what kind of riding they want to do, all the standard questions. Sometimes, he says, they really have no idea what they need and they don't listen to advice. They have a set notion of what will suit them – a replica of a pro's bike and, *ecco*, they'll turn into a Bartoli, a Rodriguez. Indeed, sometimes Pegoretti's suggestion that a cheaper frame more apt to the client sounds like an affront, as if only the most expensive can possibly be the best choice. Not true. I reflect, there's no accounting for ignorance. He smiles and adds a discursus on a familiar theme. I paraphrase: Forty years ago you had to go to a workshop, immerse yourself in building, learn it from your fingers, eyes, a sort of rhythm, you absolutely had to touch the material to know it. Now? You go to a bookshop and buy *Frame-building for Dummies* and, hey, everyone's a maestro. I tell him the story of the Americans who ask the gardener at an English stately home how long it took

ABOVE
Fatti con le mani ('made by hand') is a central tenet of the entire Pegoretti operation.

LEFT
The cartoon on the wall was a morale-booster to Dario in his fight against cancer. Since his diagnosis and treatment, he has worked with the Stuttgart State Academy of Art and Design to raise funds for a children's cancer charity.

The Catholic iconography was the inspiration of a former employee.

Dario has one foot in the traditionalists' camp and one foot in that of the modernists. Together with Richard Sachs, he has designed a tube-set that is produced by Columbus. Modern and thin-walled, the PegoRichie is built into lugs.

to produce 'a lawn like that'. Old retainer replies, coldly: 'Two hundred years of care and attention.' Dario laughs.

Knowing about his eccentric decoration of the frames, I ask him about the paintwork thing. 'Oh, for me it's a joke', he says. But, when I go through the heavy plastic strips which shield the paintshop from the dust of the shop floor and talk to Diego, it's plain that the joke is rather more than a bit of a laugh. It's part of what they call *allegria* – a fundamental joy in life, the pain of it as well as the exuberance. One of his frame colour schemes is called Guantanamo, a motif of barbed wire with blobs of sanguineous red. Not many people go for that but it does illustrate the willingness not to define *joke* as mere froth. It's a very serious matter, humour. *Finita la Commedia* doesn't

signal the fat lady singing. Dante's vision of Purgatory? *Commedia*. Balzac's cycle of trenchant novels? *Comédie Humaine*.

Pegoretti himself designs the graphics for the ornamenting of the frames and the result is a lively variety of differing schemes, all from basic pattern, some subject to reworking by Dario himself, additions and embellishment. He started the painting – with no background or training – in 2006, because they had had troubles with a contractor. His influences in style? The abstract and expressionist art of the 1960s. When the work is done, a short inscription is painted onto the inner side of one rear stay. I read 'Handmade in Italia San Alfonso 2012'. (That is, 'completed on 19 September ...' – San Alfonso's festal day.) The *Ciavete* frames are all painted by hand, following

The paintwork department is as important as the frame building section. Dario rejoices in flamboyance and the Pegoretti frame is renowned for bold, or subtle, statement in colour and graphic detail.

the inspiration of the day, intricate embroideries in paint by hand brush, marker pen, spray can … whatever he feels like using. *Ciavete* is Trentino dialect for 'don't bother about it'. If someone makes a disparaging remark about something you like, for example, you might say '*ciavete*', meaning 'who cares about *your* opinion?' The customer chooses the base colour, and each successive painting is smoothed down and then covered in a clear coat, until the final decoration is done and cast over with the thin lucency, as it were a glass. One particular technique derives from one used in the Renaissance by stucco painters of Venice. This involves applying paint with a thin metal scraper to make swirls and drifts of opposed colours as it were a fusion of chromes in wet plaster. On one frame, Dario has added an inscription, painted by hand: *Andrea e quando penso che sia finite e proprio*

allora che incomincia la salita … a reminder to the bike's owner/rider, Andrea, that it's just when you think you're done that the climb really starts. On one frame, painted in classic colours, dark maroon and classy taupe, the original Pegoretti logo, two interlocked gold Ps, and on the down tube *Luigino Milani*, in tribute to the master.

It is plain that the painting is very far from a joke, more an expression of voluptuous delight in form and finish of the bicycle frame and an open acknowledgement of the care that goes into it. Even the public jest of the kitchen wall – a notice *Vietato fumare* hovering over an ashtray crammed full of butts on the table, like a crucifix over a sybarite – has a similar wry edge. Bite.

As an apprentice to Luigi Milani, the young Dario was steeped in Italian craftsmanship and the culture of Italian frame-building.

FRAMES • Newmarket, New Hampshire, USA

Draughts from doors and windows can
disturb the flow of gas around the weld area.
IF welders sit inside shielded cubicles: Keith
Rouse has been sitting in one of these for
nine years.

INDEPENDENT FABRICATION

The nomenclature of many of New England's rivers, towns, lakes and roads has its origin in
the languages of the Native Americans who welcomed the first settlers and, at the start of
their first winter, introduced them to what became the staples of the seminal meal to celebrate
their survival, Thanksgiving: the turkey and the cranberry. The colonists left their imprint, too
– for example, in Rockingham County, New Hampshire, the towns of Newmarket, Epsom,
Durham, Northwood … echoes of the old England they had left behind. In this lovely pocket
of America, scattered with lakes, ponds and vast tracts of dense woodland, once lived the
aboriginal Abenaki, 'the people of the dawnlands'. They named the tidal estuary close to
Newmarket the Piscataqua, 'branch of a river with a strong current', and bequeathed the
glorious chirrup of Pawtuckaway Park and lake to the west. Newmarket is home, now, to
the Independent Fabrication enterprise, founded in 1995. When the pioneering mountain
bike manufacturer Fat City Cycles was declared insolvent, in 1994, the brand was sold, the
factory in Somerville, Massachusetts, left empty, the workforce disbanded. End of story?
No. Some of the ex-Fat City people, still lean and mean with ambition to design and build
custom bikes, set up a new independent company. How were they going to survive in the
harsh economic climate that had stranded them? By hard toil in a rather cramped work space
and dedication to their abiding pre-eminent trading principles: to make high-end, precise,
handcrafted frames and to allow a customer to paint his or her bike whatever colours they
asked for, even if the colours were tasteless, unsightly, garish. If the new company was going
to be independent, then the customers must be permitted the same freedom.

Filler rods racked up and ready for use. The straight rods are used for joining the tubes together while the wire on the spool is used for tacking on such items as bottle and rack mounts.

LEFT
A gas lens is used to direct the argon gas onto the welding area around the tungsten electrode and it's vital to keep the gas flowing over the joint whilst it cools. Tig welding titanium at this level is very difficult but these people make it look easy. The weld puddle is formed at temperatures well in excess of 800°C and keeping that run of liquid neat and tidy demands formidable expertise.

These are principles to which they have been faithful. A glance at some of the colour schemes that leave the more spacious works in Newmarket (to which they moved in 2011) is vibrant testimony to that. Let's single out one frame whose colouring is based on that of a cantaloupe melon in a lush, sunlit, Florida garden. *Chacun à son* … as they say.

However, there is something essentially friendly about Independent Fabrication (IF): the way they work, the business commitment, the love of the bicycle per se and the people who, reflecting that, buy and ride the bikes they make – there's even an IF Owners Club – which is entirely winsome and cheerful. Against what can become the giddying surreality of techno-babble – the delight of some, the deterrent of others – it's good to hear the downright straight talk of a mission statement which might read: Hey, guys, we really get off on what we're doing and we get off on the fact that you really like what we're doing, too. Let's ride.

Gary Smith, the founder of IF 'gave up his parking space in the rat race to make bikes and bags … [because] bikes are easier to park so who needs the reserved space?' Their chief frame builder nominates the IF BMX bike as his favourite: 'You've got to love a bike that makes you feel like a 200 pound 12 year-old.' The company co-sponsors a local 45-mile challenge and charity ride, the RAID Rockingham, and the ad. concludes: 'Join us for the after-party featuring Smuttynose beer, good food and lots of swag to give away. So, sign up – we'd be honored to show you our local roads and secret stash of packed gravel.' They quite clearly revel in the fun, the sheer exuberance of riding a bike, whether it be cross-country or roads. The RAID is a community gig – it raises money for the Franklin County Land Trust.

The spirit of high jinks comes out in a very individual approach to design. Some egregious examples: the black frame with delicate red ribboning which nods at the coachwork of a classic Fiat 500 model and the inexpressibly elegant, fine-boned, single-speed, steel frame town bike which takes its aesthetic inspiration from the petrol driven 1914 Indian board track racer (petrol-driven bikes for races on tracks like velodromes, no brakes,

During welding the tubes are purged with argon gas. The weld area is also shielded with the gas to prevent oxidisation and to obviate joint failure.

Heavyweight machinery sits alongside the lightweight machinery and hand tools.

Cleanliness is very important when welding titanium. Grease, moisture and even sweat may oxidise in the heat of the weld and react with the titanium and/or the filler rod and thereby compromise the integrity of the joint.

Tolerances and quality control are very tight.

clutch, transmission or accelerator, speeds up to 100mph. They called the short tracks with banking of 50° 'murder dromes'.) The beautiful, slender cadre is enhanced by lustrous embellishment. Smith is 'a bit of a parts pack rat, always acquiring and saving things for the right build'. For this bike he reserved a titanium headset with walnut inlay (one of a limited run he bought from Cane Creek a while ago), a Rolls saddle from his stash and, like a benediction, a chivalric blazon, the logo and name on the down tube in gold leaf. Eschewing brash, common or garden gold paint, they experimented, not too successfully, with an amateur gold leaf kit from a DIY store. Then, by the kind of serendipity which often blesses the eccentric, Smith met a professional gilder who came to the workshop and left a touch of magic with real 24-carat gold leaf. This goes beyond fancy, this is de luxe. Another bike, custom-built for an ardent fisherman, an adventure, all-terrain machine that would convey him to the most secret fishing holes, has a colour scheme melding shades of purple, green and blue hues that 'shift in an out of the bottom fade' like the back of a river trout. And what of the sweet jest in planting bar end caps on the El Fabuloso MTB 'featuring flying monkey skulls wearing IF crowns'?

Smith's credo, that of IF, a belief that frame building does and must fuse art with science, 'alchemist meets engineer', is that their customers 'expect us to be obsessed with the little things and I believe that we have an obligation as professionals to never stop caring about the small details that add up to something more than just another consumable product'. Let's ignore the split infinitive and instance the special finish they gave to a bike for 'an intrepid world traveller' who wanted plain steel, no paint. Normally, painting a frame requires three phases: 1. laying on a primer that etches chemically into the bare metal; 2. a base coat to carry the colour; 3. a top coat of clear varnish to protect and give a glossy shine. For bare steel, they needed to find a clear epoxy primer that would bond chemically with the steel and be able to take a clear coat finish.

The IF designers and makers strive constantly to keep up to date, deploying the newest metal technologies as well as in the refinement of accepted techniques. Yet, although the advent of titanium and carbon fibre has led to a greater sophistication of production methods, they still make bikes by hand, with the utmost respect for traditional craftsmanship. Of course, other frame builders use the same high-end metals and components. But, says Smith, 'it's how we transform them that set us apart. It's the beauty of design and the flawlessness of the welds'. That's it: independent in name, spirit and practice.

Gary Smith 'the main man'.

Chris Rowe, lead painter and the 'James Brown of paint'.

Pre paint inspection.

Ti, carbon and Campag' truly a thing of beauty. Form and function.

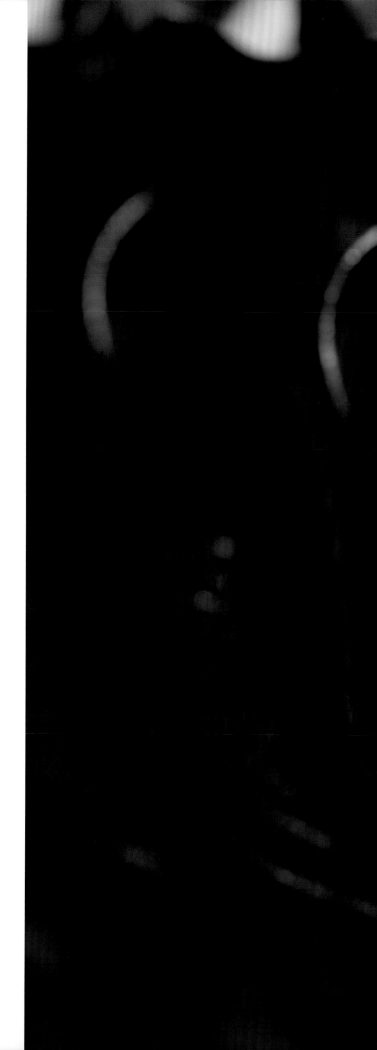

FRAMES • Warwick, Massachusetts, USA

Dropouts, fork ends and crowns bear the distinctive stamp of this most individual of makers.

'Because technology alone is a poor substitute for experience.'

RICHARD SACHS

In a spotless, white-painted workshop (a converted double garage) amply lit by natural light, not far from the Connecticut River in that state, a Thoreau-esque New England backwoods idyll, Richards Sachs has been making bike frames, to his own specification, since 1975. He attended a Yeshiva – Rabbinical school – in the early grades and seemed, when he left the senior school, destined for a career in writing and journalism. But, he'd been smitten with bike racing and with bike racing came the hankering for the sleek machine, the goblin-silver components, the wheels, so frail in look, so strong in use. Hence his constant trips to the treasure trove that was Kopp's Cycles near Princeton which seeded a growing desire to do something with bicycles. 'What drew me in', he said, 'was the combination of a beautiful sport with beautiful bikes. They spoke to me and they were used for racing.'

He took a temporary job in Manhattan, read an advertisement for a bike mechanic in a shop in Vermont and, two days later, was on the Greyhound for the six-hour ride. What else was he going to do? Phone? The job was already taken, and he had no experience or training. Sorry, pal. He has said that the rejection was a bit humiliating. 'But within a day I had devised a scheme to redeem myself. If fixing bicycles was cool, then making bicycles had to be cool squared.' A clutch of letters to frame builders in Britain – his labour without pay in return for training – three replies, one said 'come' and so he came, to Witcomb Lightweight Cycles in Deptford, by the Thames, where the diarist John Evelyn grew lettuces all year round, near the shipyard where Peter the Great of Russia learnt to build vessels for his navy and Ferranti lit The Light (the power station) with his new system of electricity. The eighteen-year-old Sachs

"The workshop is no place for a neophyte".

Lathered in flux awaiting the heat. The flux facilitates the brazing process by cleaning the joint chemically, thus preventing oxidisation and encouraging the filler material to flow into the joint much like hot glue. Richard uses an alloyed filler rod that is 56 per cent silver.

Richard Sachs prefers to work alone. His workshop is a quiet, contemplative place dedicated to the practice of excellence.

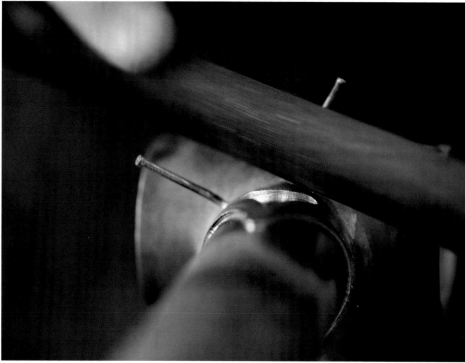

Despite his fame, Richard Sachs is a modest and self-effacing man who acknowledges that there's always more to learn.

Asked about tig welding, Richard's answer is short and sweet: 'I've never welded ... the question went over my head.'

His own self-imposed control of what he makes is uncompromising.

wrote to his Mom: 'Bikes are what I forsee [sic] myself being in for a long while to come and I think coming here was the break of my lifetime.'

At Witcomb, as he describes it, 'I was baptised in a work environment (typical of the day) in which there were no fixtures – none. There were drawing tables that allowed the staff to compare cut tubes with design parameters and the horizon [no slant-tubed bikes back then]. The tables had well-worn scribed lines representing angles, setback, lengths, and frame drop. There were also some spring clamps and angle iron around that allowed for some primitive holding of parts kept in plane by hardware store quality straight edges, a complete absence of power tools. Everything was brazed against a well-assembled wall of firebricks. It was the best learning environment for me. If you can't feel, discern, use intuition, or listen to the material, all the quality control checks and dial indicators in the world will add misery to the process.'

Of course he does apply the most rigorous checks on his frames but there is only one power tool, a battery-driven electric drill, in the silent workshop where he works alone. He's introspective. A devout loner ... an admitted control freak ... all extraneous noise excluded. Silence carries 'the sound of my own thoughts ... I can hear my own voice clearly without interruption. When I work alone it's me the metal and the heat and we work out this little passion play between us.' Three to five days to make one frame.

His own self-imposed control of what he makes is uncompromising. 'I make

the bike, you have to ride it' – that is you have to be fit enough to ride it, for racing. This ain't for neophytes. Options lead to insanity, customising means competition, so, concentrate on one form and make it well. This in the context of a very singular approach to the construction of a frame using the Pegorichie steel tubing, which he developed in conjunction with the celebrated frame-builder Dario Pegoretti in 2005. This tubing is made from Columbus' unique nivacom micro-alloyed steel with manganese, chrome, nickel, molybdenum and niobium, and offers better mechanical properties and greater resistance to atmospheric corrosion than conventional carbon steels.

Sachs is a man of intense devotion to the work to which he came early but which took him a long time to assimilate – he calculates that he wasn't really settled as a frame-maker until he had built some 1,000. The reason? His uncertainty in the technique. Of the days at Witcomb, he recalls, 'framebuilders were also metal-smiths, artisans, not simply joiners and assemblers as we have become these days. Though working with the torch was generally left to the most senior members of a framebuilding concern's staff, the preparation and reworking of all the little fittings was carried out by the apprentices. This is how we cut our teeth in those days. The quality of even the finest components was so poor that, unless one developed the skills to reshape, file, fit, re-fit, and thin – unless one had the hands and eyes to discern the right clearance and proper aesthetics – no piece would get far enough along in the building process for the masters to be able to perform their magic.'

His relationship to a frame is highly sensual, responding to touch, feel, its wholeness. As a bike racer who builds frames (not the other way round) he insists, too, that frame-building is a lot more than a mere mechanical process. It partakes of the rider, the essence of the person for whom it is made. A bad fit makes a bad ride. It offends taste. Some of his dicta (expressed as ATMO, 'according to my opinion', the nickname he uses) have a near mystical echo: learning to build a frame is easy … learning to build frames is not that easy, the two processes are polar opposites. However, unpick the sense and here is the kernel of his solitary, uncluttered work. Individuation. A passion for things beautifully made by hand. He quotes the painter Balthus, contemplating finely carved wooden shingles on a cabin roof and praising 'the trouble the [joiners] took for something that could not even be seen. That is what has been lost. It was lost when workers began selling their time. Or, as you say in America, when time became money.'

Sachs, whose purist approach makes him, he says, 'the Devil's devil's advocate', had his own gloss on the incurious, factory-based, mass-produced method which replaced handcraft in the '80s: 'Ours is a plug-in, cookie cutter-like industry now. Save for the tube-set, every single component for the frame-builder is now available in the antiseptic-like, model room quality that comes from the wax molds of the foundries of a few different firms. It is a Rollerball society for frame-building … Inhale crude, exhale cast.'

If this sounds grumpy, it probably is, but it's the grump of a man whose high ideals and exactitude may be summed up in his own assessment: 'Neither the lug, [he makes templates in plasticine/clay and files and sands by hand] the alignment, the geometry, the materials, constitute the frame. The frame is the frame … a totality, a concept realised in the work of the craftsman's hand, unique as each human being is unique. Every object made by hand carries its own blessing, its own mark, the invisible imprint of the hand that shaped it. That demands a special focus.' Sachs puts it thus: *'All that matters is what you think. If you ever second guess yourself, pause until you don't.'*

He asks clients to place their order in January – that makes his administrative labour easier – warns them it's a seven-year wait, takes three to five days to build a frame and, firm on the principle that it's not just work at the bench that counts but stopping to stare, too, he can look out through the big frame glass doors on Golden Pond. Visitors? Hm, not cool and if one does make it inside: *Keep your hand off the wall… who knows what grime or alien matter you'll plant there.*

Sachs is a very thoughtful, articulate man with sharp and considered insight into the craft he practises. His blogs delve deep into its mystery and he celebrates its mystery with an inner delight, a celebration of 'actual rather than perceived quality'.

Hours of cutting and sanding go into every Sachs job. There are no short cuts, no automation, only files, emery paper and intense concentration.

The only power tool Richard uses is a battery operated drill: muscle memory and skill are the elements that set his frames apart. As he says '… technology alone is a poor substitute for experience'.

The original order book. Sachs is as meticulous in his record keeping as he is in making the frames. A matter of pride in him.

Road bike or cyclo cross, it's your choice. Whichever bike you go for, you're assured of the best.

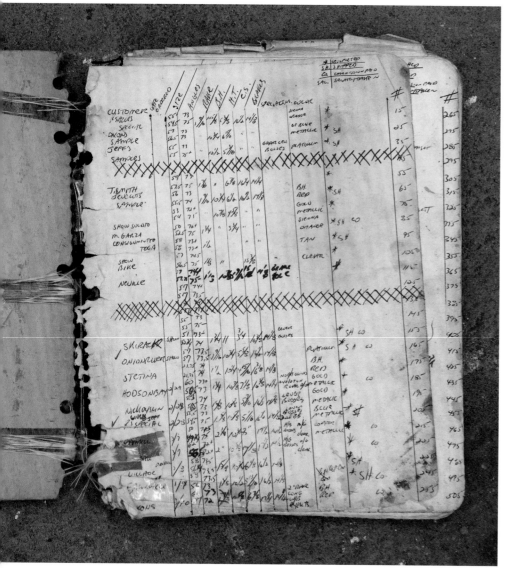

Masterly heat control is crucial to maintaining the strength of a joint in the thinnest tubing. Too hot and the tubing can burn, too cold and the solder will not flow. The trick is to apply heat to the thicker lug or the dropout, for example, to allow the heat to transfer thence to the thinner tube.

A masterpiece in miniature.

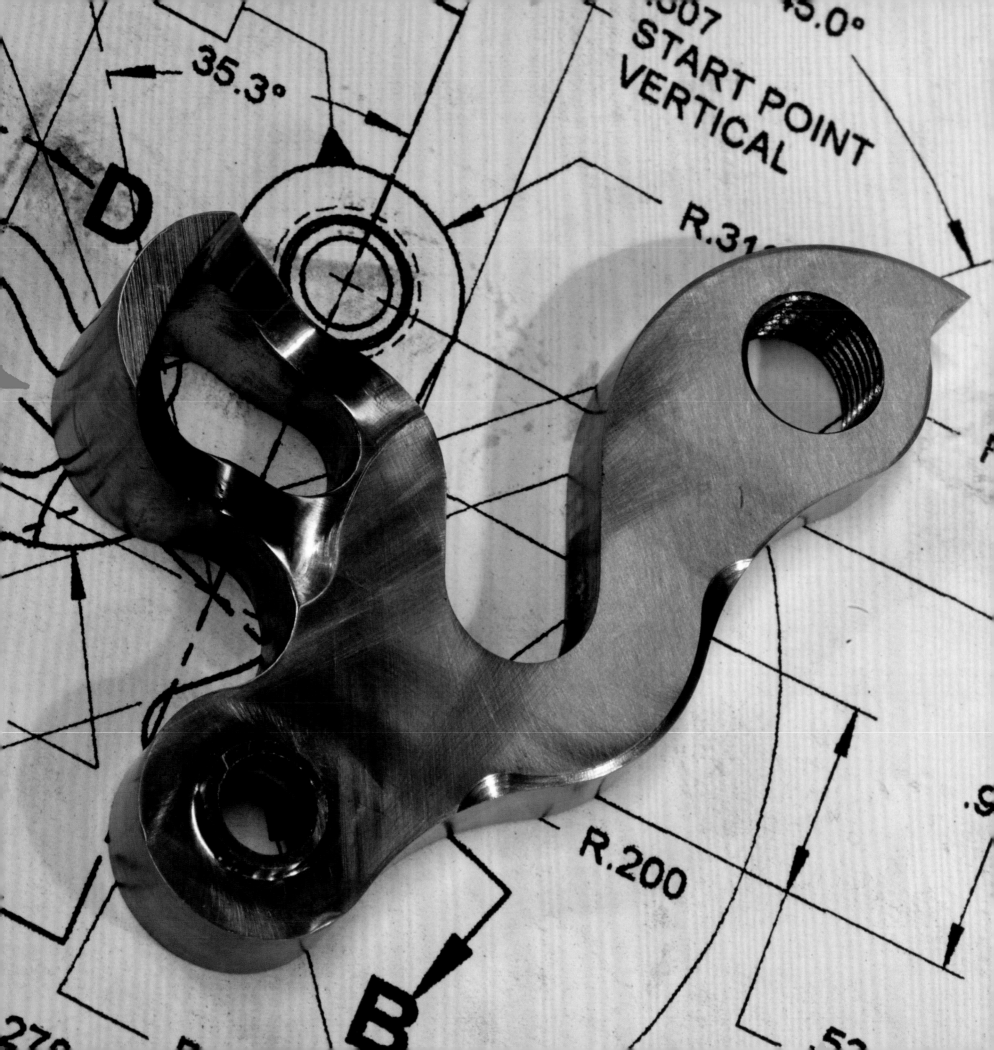

BEN SEROTTA

Ben Serotta is one of four American frame-builders who trained in the Witcomb Lightweight workshop during the 1970s. In 1928, Tom Witcomb, a steel worker in the Thames-side dockyards, built his first bicycle frames in the cellar of his east London house. There is something of a tradition for what one might call such backroom enterprise in Britain – men with a passion working on the kitchen table, in a garden shed, a cluttered store room. Tom's son Ernie expanded the business and, in 1952, began trading as Witcomb Lightweight Cycles. His son, Barrie started his apprenticeship as a frame-builder in 1958 at the age of 15. It became a Mecca for cyclists who wanted the best there could be had.

Ben Serotta described the workshop when he arrived as like something out of Dickens, a real dingy, chilly, antiquated cave of making. The industrial unrest of the time, the three-day week, meant that they often had to work by candlelight. There was no concession to comfort. The warmest place was the pub around the corner. All the frames were preheated on a bed of coal to encourage the solder and flux to flow evenly round the lugs.

The Serotta works in Saratoga is worlds apart. Clean as a surgery, airy, spacious and dedicated to a near obsessive shaping of frames for individual need and a scrupulous even geekish scientific method of sizing and shaping. For, at the extremes, there are two approaches to fitting a frame to a rider. There are those makers who will measure the whole body, the morphology of a potential rider, even, one suspects, to the length of the fingers. A person's height does not necessarily indicate the proportion of leg length to that of the upper body, and so on … minute distinctions which must be accommodated. Contrariwise, as Alice

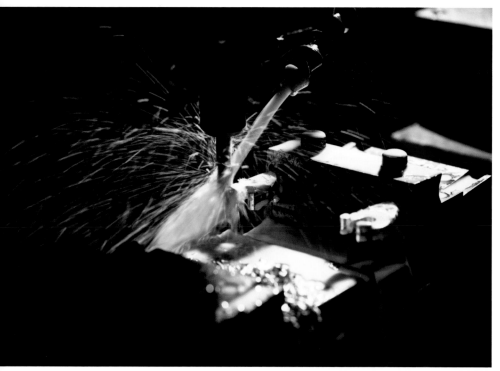

TOP LEFT
Dropouts, fork ends and other such items are CNC machined in house.

ABOVE
Rough edges are knocked off in a tumbling vat of ceramic chips.

LEFT
An early head badge design.

A separate facility dedicated to carbon supplies Serotta with tubing, shells and lugs. These are worked and assembled in the Saratoga factory. Here we see glue being applied to the tubes before they are slotted together.

Alignment in a jig is critical; cold setting a carbon frame is not an option.

The bottom bracket shell before and after machining.

The Tour of the Battenkill is an event local to Serotta and an excellent proving ground for the bikes ... and for Scott Hock, a Serotta employee and passionate bicycle maker.

would say, there is the opinion that all this pernicketiness is bunkum, that all a real builder needs to do is look, to size up the rider by eye. Everything follows. When King George I visited his Royal Naval Dockyard at Chatham, on the Medway, he remarked irritably of a man who stood stock still, staring at a woodshed, 'Shouldn't he be working?' The Master Boatbuilder said, firmly and with deference, 'But he is working, your Majesty ... he's sizing and selecting the timber.' With a trained eye. (What the Master Boatbuilder thought privately of His Hanoverian Snottiness is not recorded.)

However, there are as many opinions abroad as people to express them and Serotta's mantra is: *I make the bike for you*. To this end, he has his own swaging facility to ... but, wait. Swaging, I hear you say, what is swaging? Swage can mean the excrement of an otter but in its derivation from assuage, to appease, relieve, reduce, the word describes the shaping or bending or reduction in size of generally cold but sometimes hot metal with a special tool or by forcing it into a die or mould. Serotta manipulates the form of titanium and steel tubes to give them different characteristics – for

instance thicker at the ends, which imparts stiffness, thinner in the middle which lends flexibility. The thicker metal takes a weld more readily and gives strength and integrity to the joint. The down tube, because it carries the rider's weight directly, needs to be very stiff. Serotta also uses carbon, produced by a separate facility in California.

Saratoga in upstate New York is the town where General John Burgoyne surrendered to his American counterpart, General Horatio Gates, on 17 October, 1777; a British defeat often reckoned to have led to final victory for the United States in the American Revolutionary War. Ben Serotta has his own take on revolutions – of pedals and of concepts, both.

'One of my many issues is that I think all my ideas are brilliant', he says with a smile indicating that he knows this isn't true. However, he adds, 'In my core there's a desire to leave something special behind'. The most obvious innovatory side of the Serotta concern is the Fit Lab where customers are assessed both as riders and individuals. The common conception is that a

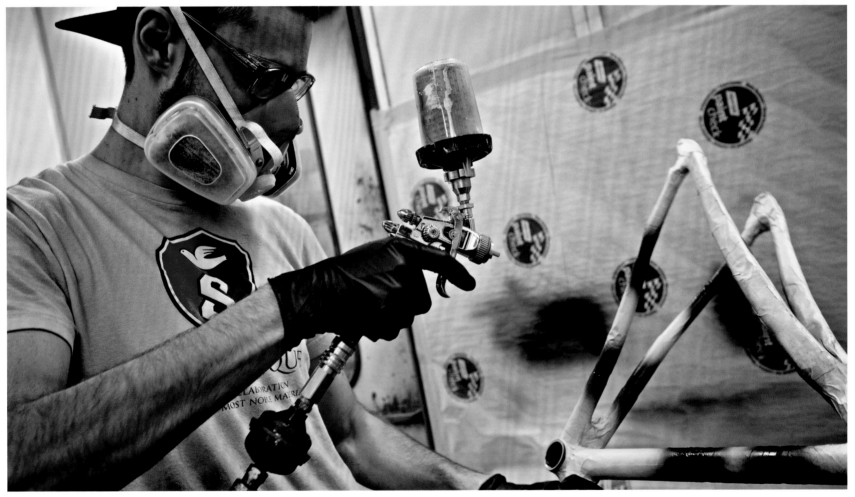

Working hard in the spray booth, a dust free, temperature controlled environment.

ABOVE LEFT

Ben Serotta: 'We want to build the best bike for you. And the best bike is the bike that makes you want to go out and ride it.'

The Colorado Concept was developed for the 1984 USA Olympic team's bikes but is now common throughout the range. It involves shaping and manipulating the individual tubes of a bike frame to specific purpose.

Serotta build in steel, carbon and titanium. They have their own carbon production facilities and swage their own steel tubing to their own specification. Ben Serotta is particularly excited by the possibilities offered by carbon.

custom-built bike emerges from geometry and measurement. At the Serotta Fit Lab, however, the rider sits on a special machine, hip, knee and ankle marked with a detectable patch which can then be observed on a screen monitor as he or she turns the cranks. The angles opening as the leg flexes give indication of the nature of the rider's pedal stroke and offers essential clues into what differentiates him or her from the customer who proceeds or follows them in. The laboratory director, Steven LeBoyer, says 'We look at a fit, not just a bunch of numbers, certainly not a formula. It's a process, we really get to know each rider.' He adds that when riders leave, they've also been educated, because they not only get the right fitting but they're walked through the way it was achieved. Bespoke is a much-overused word these days but a Serotta is, truly, a bespoke bicycle. Serotta reckons to have produced between 40,000–60,000 bikes since the beginning and he guesses that half of them will still be in service … like a bespoke pair of hob-formed shoes, a fitted suit.

It came, he said, 'from a light bulb moment'. Ben was drinking beer with a doctor friend, poring over a copy of Gray's anatomy (staple reading for medical students) in the hope of bolstering his own hands-on expertise with some science. His friend told him this was misguided. 'You can't treat the body as a machine' he said, 'you must look at the cyclist as a whole.'

Until then the standard fitting technique was to take the Italian (*Coni*) handbook and translate or adapt that for a client. Thus, if a customer was 6 foot tall, he'd get a bike that measured 60cm in the seat tube because that's what a six foot tall gold medallist had ridden. You did get a stem of your choice. But a bike is not a simple tool, like a hammer, a mere linear extension of your body, it moves in multiple dimensions.

Serotta is persuasive about his belief. "Everyone says they want to build the best bikes in the world. I take this further and say I understand it better. We want to build the best bikes for you, bikes you'll want to ride more and often. A comfortable bike will allow any cyclist to perform better. Comfort and endurance go hand in hand. We all have our own vision of the perfect bike based on our memories and our heroes. Whilst it's still gratifying to build a bike which is balanced aesthetically, the most beautiful thing is actually successful cycling. We build bikes to be ridden and ridden hard by whoever, wherever.'

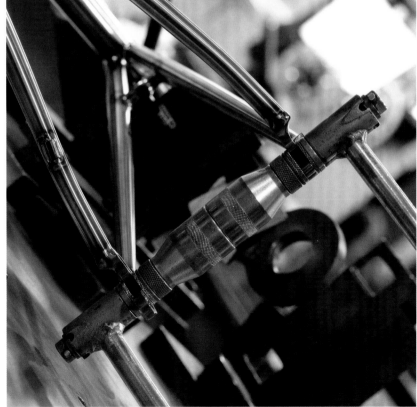

Founded in 1972, Serotta can call on an impressive pool of talent in their small, highly skilled, highly motivated work force on the shop floor.

FRAMES • Grays Inn Road, London, UK

Monty Young is an accomplished wheel builder and was responsible for drilling the wooden rims seen in the bike build. They're a special order item.

CONDOR/PARIS

Condor: Spanish version of *kuntur*, its name in the tongue of the Quechua Indians. One of the largest birds in the world, wing span of up to ten feet [3.05 metres], native to the High Andes, an important symbol in Inca mythology.

When Napoleon, having escaped from Elba, landed near Antibes on the southern coast of France on 1 March 1815, with an 800-strong bodyguard, he made his way north on what has, ever since, been known as the Route Napoléon. Alluding to the finial atop his regimental banners, he boasted that 'the eagle will fly from steeple to steeple until he reaches the towers of Notre Dame'.

And then came a Condor over Paris.

The legendary founder of Condor Cycles (*Our claim to fame is in the name* – its first advertising slogan), Monty Young, learnt his skills in bicycle mechanics, from the age of fifteen, in the workshop of Harry "Spanner" Rensch of Stoke Newington, in London. Rensch had been in the bike trade since before the War, changed the name of his business to Paris around 1942 – his name sounded too German – and was a celebrated innovator. His frames, very popular among the serious racing fraternity, were ultra light, classy of line, even somewhat odd in structure. The Paris 'Galibier' had a curiously configured arrangement of tubes forming the lower part of the frame, designed to eliminate 'whip' but imparting a certain elasticity which made for better road holding.

After the War, Young teamed up with his new brother-in-law, Walter Conway, who had secured the agency for Triumph Cycles in London and opened a shop in Gray's Inn Road. He was the businessman, Monty the Rensch-inspired mechanic, who very soon felt the itch to construct his own bikes, not to deal in ready-made stuff from Coventry. But what to call the

new marque? Conway? Conway and Young? Hm, dull. What about a bird, to symbolise power and speed? A motorcycle (later bicycle) manufacturer in Coventry had bagged the eagle in 1897...Falcon was hovering close ... Cuckoo? Come on, concentrate. Concentrate ... back to Conway ... Con-something ... Con ... DOR. Open sesame. 1948.

1981

Young decided that the tradition of the Paris bicycles should be revived and continued. (The original company had succumbed to commercial pressures and been dissolved in 1955. Rensch died in 1984.) This renaissance of Paris under Young's aegis is a measure of his utter commitment to the joy of cycling (although his first sporting love was weight-lifting) and the highest standards of design and manufacture of the beautiful machine. Rensch's frames were singular in that, unlike most frames of the time, his used no lugs. A lug, a collar into which two tubes can be welded, allows for a certain leeway in fabrication tolerances. Rensch used bronze welding to join the tubes and, for the head tube, a Gothic style bi-lamination. Translated into English, this describes a finely cut sleeve of thin metal wrapped round the head tube in precise fit, one at the top, another at the bottom and then fused with it. This process, now better known as Sif-bronze brazing, requires a more controlled technique – an exceptional expertise from cutting out of the metal sheet through to the play of flame and weld – but makes for a stronger frame than one constructed with lugs and brass brazing.

The intricate work needed to fashion the bi-lamination and the dearth of requisite skills necessarily restricted the Condor output of Paris lightweight frames. There was a year-long waiting list for every one of them. The tubing was upgraded to a super lightweight steel heat-treated for tensile strength. But the masterly welding, cutting and testing techniques had to be learned by a new generation of artisans and the emergence of Condor/Paris frames from their subterranean workshop was and remains slow.

In late 2008 Grant, Monty's son and boss of Condor, decided to bring the Paris frames up to date and make them as accessible as they had been in their first incarnation ... using new construction methods to reduce the build time. After two years of research, Condor invested in bang up-to-date laser cutting technology, just as Rensch had looked to the latest technology in his day to build his performance racing machines. The latest models of the range made by Condor – the *Paris Path* and *Paris Road* – introduced in 2011, feature a handmade, lightweight, fillet-brazed frame of tubing in steel alloyed with manganese and vanadium, the distinctive bi-laminations cut with lasers and a frame livery with a retro style. All the rage these days.

It is a thing of beauty, the Condor/Paris. Still no more than thirty of them are being made per annum but, for their sleekness of line, their heritage of class, their lovely down-sweep handlebars, their spare elegance, each one is a rare thing of beauty.

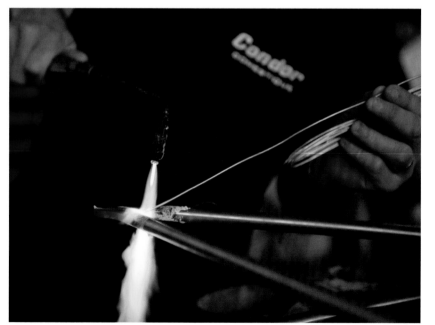

Keeping the flame alive. Lugged and bi-laminated joints are painstakingly and skilfully executed. They say that time is money, that's why a hand built frame is not cheap. It's reassuring.

TOP LEFT
Depending on the model, fixtures like bottle cage bosses are added.

TOP CENTRE
Northern Italy has more than its fair share of workshops. They're quiet, efficient and productive.

TOP RIGHT
News from the trade in 1947. The Galibier model, shown in the picture, caused quite a stir because of the new principles of frame design which it incorporated. Claims included resistance to the whiplash caused by pedalling, along with built-in elasticity to counter road shock.

LEFT
A dedicated production facility in Italy handles the frame building. Fathers, sons, brothers and cousins are all involved and the workshop is steeped in tradition.

RIGHT
The bi-laminated head lug and badge is a thing of
both strength and beauty.

Well established family firms usually have a much
loved and well used child's bike somewhere in the
back room. Whilst they make great wall art, they
sometimes look like they're crying out to be taken
out and used.

ABOVE
The expected collection
of files and abrasives
used to finish off joints,
clean seat and head
tubes and rub down any
contamination.

RIGHT
Expert assembly means
that the effort which
the framebuilder has
put into the bike isn't
in vain. Sweating the
details all the way
through the production
process gives a much
better end result.

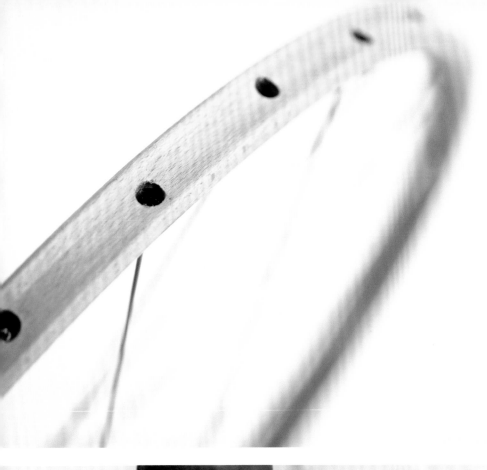

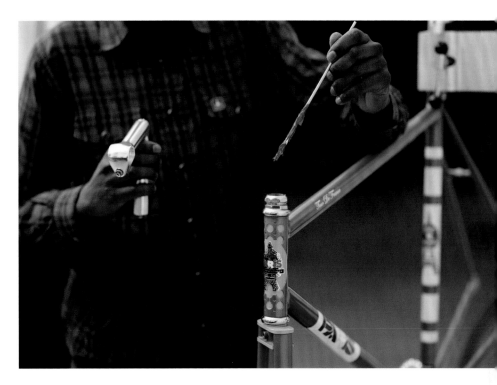

TOP LEFT
Wooden rims are probably best saved for the velodrome or the concours competition. Layers of beech offer a lightweight and 'springy' rim which although gives a comfortable ride also means that power is lost from the pedalling action.

ABOVE
A dab of grease and a quill stem. What else?

LEFT
From Northern Italy to London, the journey of this Paris is almost finished.

"The only thing better than Sevens are the Sevens we haven't built yet. It's exciting to be a part of that."
Seven Cycles employee

SEVEN

In Watertown, a small community to the west of Boston city, Massachusetts, the people of Seven Cycles work and have their being. They ride bikes, they make bikes, they develop new ideas for bikes, they love what they do and they have a winsome customer focus. 'One bike. Yours', they say, insisting that, 'this isn't simply a slogan. It represents the heart of our philosophy about who we are and what we do. And nowhere is this philosophy more apparent than in our manufacturing. At Seven, each craftsperson focuses on only one bike at a time. Yours.'

The impression of a slightly New Age approach in this would not be wholly awry. They are – and it's difficult to avoid the sense that Sevens Cycles is, indeed, an amalgam of all its individual parts, much as the bicycle is per se bicycle itself – very open about the emotional attachment to their business. Does this in part stem from riding in the lovely lanes around Boston, the Dover and Wellesley areas, the leafy roads of Lexington and Concord and Walden Pond, even before the brilliant chromes of Fall paint the trees? I've ridden them myself and would say it does. But, there is no whimsy about their trade.

'Consider our proprietary tube butting technologies. We hold the wall thickness variations to within 0.001"—less than the thickness of a human hair. Because even a 0.001" deviation can create a 5 per cent difference in that tube's ride characteristics within the frame. Then there's our obsession with frame alignment. Every Seven frame is subjected to no less [*i.e. fewer*] than 50 alignment checks—28 in welding alone. Each is designed to guarantee the straightest, most accurate frame possible. It's no small effort to hold tolerances as tight as

ABOVE
Titanium, almost half the weight of steel and more than twice as heavy as aluminum, is around three times stronger than both.

RIGHT
Titanium is said to have been discovered in Cornwall (UK) in 1791 by William Gregor. Its corrosion resistance, high fatigue life and resilience make it ideal for a bicycle frame.

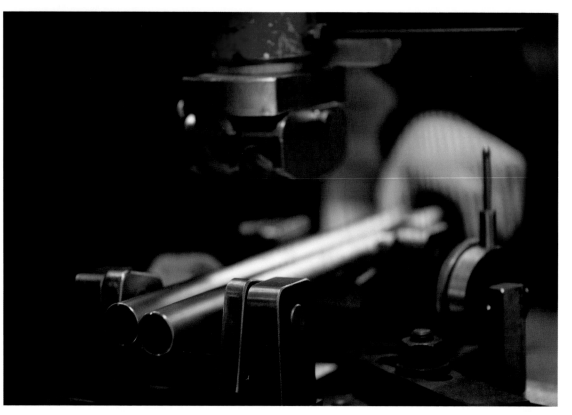

Everyone at Seven is dedicated and passionate, matching the enthusiasm of the cottage industry builder with the imperatives of the full production line factory.

Seven 'build one bike at a time ... your bike'. Since 1997 the team has been designing, refining and customising for the discerning cyclist.

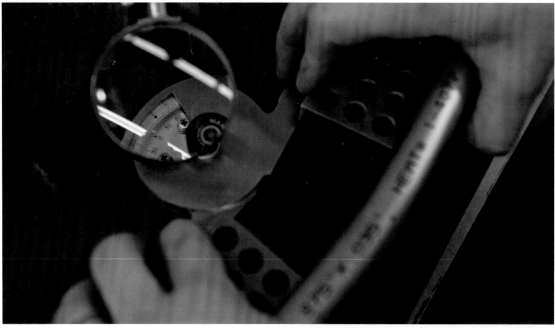

RIGHT
Welders at Seven are artists and engineers. Their job demands intense concentration.

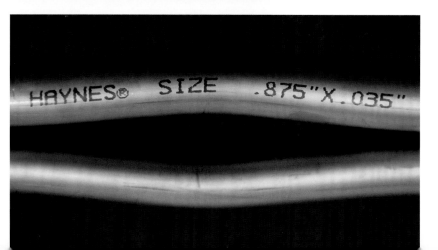

+/- 0.002" for the most critical measurements. (That's thinner than a sheet of paper.) But it's crucial to ensuring proper bike handling. Why do we go to such extremes? Creating the best possible ride characteristics is one reason. A passion to push the bounds of what's possible is another.'

It's really no surprise that in a recent interview, a member of the company drew a direct spiritual line from an early maker of bicycles, Charles Metz, who, in 1893, joined the Waltham Watch Company just along the road from the Seven premises from where he developed racing bikes and, after the death of two riders in a race on the Waltham Bicycle Park, the following year, concentrated on safety bicycles. (He went on to pioneer the manufacture of motorcycles, for pacing on velodromes.) Safety is a mission espoused energetically by Seven. The company is affiliated to a number of associations seeking to promote the wider use of bikes in America, the bike as a sustainable means of transportation, the bicycle as a vector of social change, among them *Bikes Belong, Bikes-Not-Bombs* … as well as serving on the Massachusetts Bicycle and Pedestrian Advisory Board. 'Because while a custom Seven may help you ride faster, organisations like these may help you ride longer.' (Everything is fatigue tested in house.) It's a thoughtful ideology and expressed with admirable simplicity.

To this they add an overt concern for the environment. They use petroleum-free rather than oil-based cutting fluids, for example, even though oil-based do not wear machine tools as quickly. It's a fair trade-off. They employ a special paint system that makes it possible to reuse solvents, to recycle paint waste, and to reduce to almost nothing noxious fumes and derivative particulates [tiny pieces of solid or liquid held in suspension]. This they do from choice, there is no legal requirement. When they ship a frame, it's held firmly in place in the box by a special insert, instead of the more usual mountain of packing material. This is good citizenship which they equate to the mode of building a Seven. 'It's not about doing only what is required. It's about doing what is right.'

Of the quality of Seven bikes, opinion is pretty well unanimous: they are very good. One reviewer wrote: 'The ride quality, handling and fit were as precisely tailored to my desires as a suit from a Savile Row tailor.' Whilst they do occupy an identifiable middle ground in the range of frame-making, the epithet bespoke is not out of place. One of their welders has worked as a sculptor in metal and they employ freelance machinists, as and when they're needed. Not only that, but any member of staff is allowed to work freelance, using the company machinery.

Employees are encouraged to experiment with their own projects and they are allowed to use company equipment to build frames under their own name. Such peripheral experience is valuable and cannot but enrich the Seven product.

Rob Vandermark builds beautiful bikes but he's very much a realist. He wants to build beautiful bikes that work and, perhaps more importantly, bikes which get used.

It is, for sure, a very happy place, and the Seven crowd are a very happy bunch. The fraternity of the bike? Who can gainsay that? Further, they have a strong ethic of internal company collaboration. In expressing what they see as the importance of discussion, the pooling of intelligence and theory, one even apologises for 'going a bit arty' in quoting the poet Robert Frost's famous poem 'The Road Not Taken'. Why not? It tells an important truth.

Two roads diverged in a wood and I –
I took the one less travelled by
And that has made all the difference.

Be restless, don't accept existing methods unchallenged, strive for freshness, newness, test ideas, even if they seem whacky and ridiculous, push the limits of experience and knowledge in order to 'learn stuff that we wouldn't otherwise learn'. It's a central creed.

To foster company involvement, to encourage and adopt the best ideas they can from every member of the staff who all ride to work. A good few of them are or have been racers, too. They even sponsor a small team.

Rob Vandermark founded Seven because he wanted to make custom-built bicycles. A graduate of Boston School of Art and Massachusetts Arts School, he studied sculpture and bronze casting. For him, building bikes is the perfect marriage of two passions: art and cycling. He is another deprecator of drooling over bedizened componentry, cyclists fetishising materials and divorcing the thing from its use. Whereas Vandermark does 90 per cent of the product development, individual bikes are designed by an in-house team in consultation with each individual customer.

Why Seven? The considered answer, from Rob: '"Seven" is our chosen name because it is a time-honored number that holds positive connotations all over the world and no specific attachments to other objects. This choice is important since our product is one that is sold globally. We chose a word, like a product, for which we could set the standard. We sought a name that would be as timeless, ageless, and positive as the products they would create.'

The pithy answer? Because their goal is to sell Seven bikes on all seven continents.

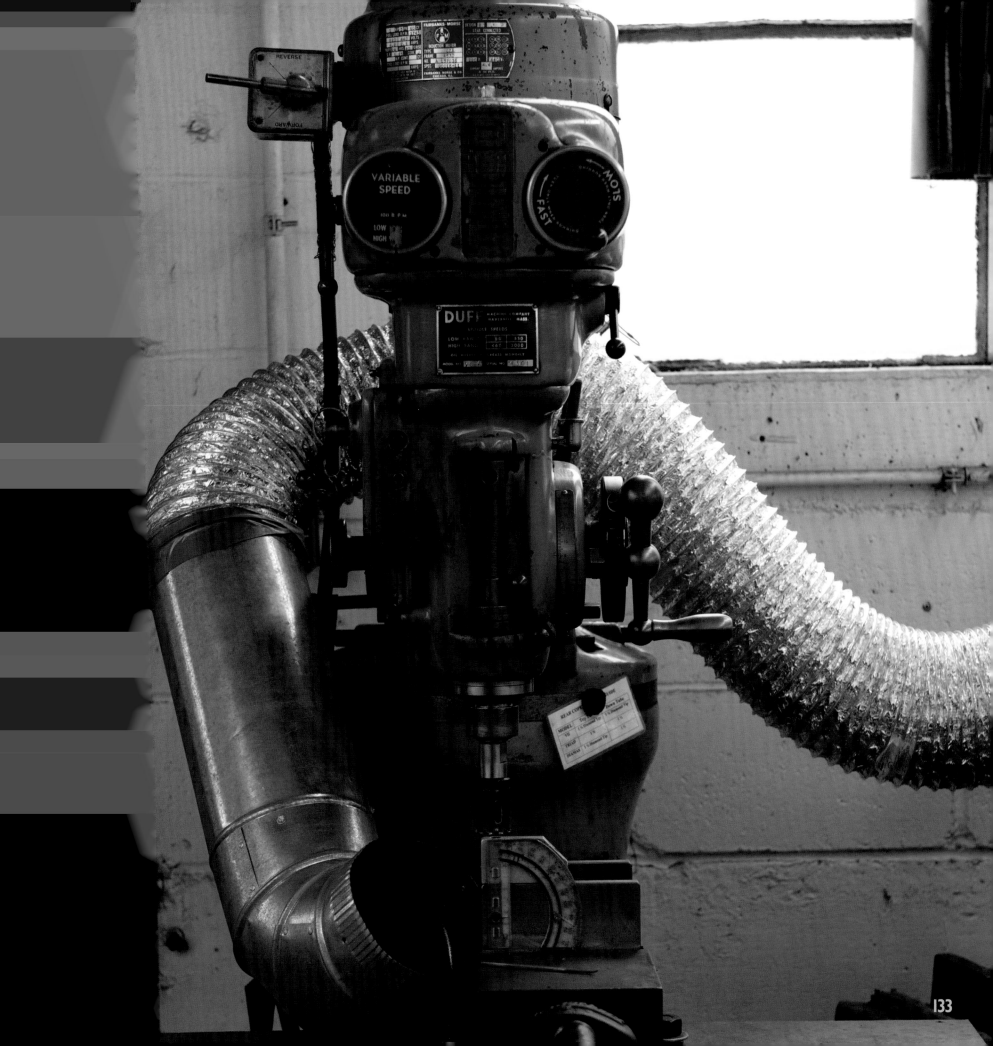

FRAMES • Sisters, Oregon, USA

Mark broke his collarbone in his first race – he came off on a bend. He used his time off the bike to evaluate why his machine didn't take the corners as well as the others.

DINUCCI

West of the mighty Blue Mountains range, the last formidable obstacle which the American pioneers tackled on the Oregon Trail, the historic route linking the Missouri River to the Oregon valleys and the Pacific coast, in a large house on a hill in the middle of nowhere, Mark DiNucci has returned to the work he began as an enthusiast without prior knowledge: building frames, making bikes. If that ain't a fair echo of pioneer, I don't know what is.

He's a very private individual, his profile on the website is blank, his house is full of stuff, cluttering the floor space and the workshop is just as bad, as if he doesn't want to throw anything away, that the orts and discards are part of an informing evolutionary process, evidence of where the stuff came from and a pointer to where it's going … like a pioneer trail map.

The first frame he built – and the first ever in Portland, Oregon – he brazed together in his 'Mom's backyard' in 1971. It took time to get things right and he clearly worked on a mix of instinct, desire and native intelligence, because the frames have become a byword for *very special* indeed. The declaration of his ideal emphasises his own reaching for what he feels to be a perfection, and feel has a lot to do with it. *Can't say maybe exactly why it's right, just feels right* may not impress some techno geeks but in some quarters it's the one thing that does count. He works without the usual array of tools and says it's crazy, it takes him so long to build a frame, but, 'whenever possible, I design every element of your frame, from fit and geometry to tubes, lugs, dropouts and fork crowns. I run a small, one-man shop where every lug is shaped, brazed and filed by me. What I do takes time and only a limited number of DiNucci frames will be made each year. I strive to deliver a frame that is as perfectly crafted as possible and I think the end product is worth the wait.'

He spent some time working with *Strawberry*, moved on to *Specialized* and, when gasoline hit a dollar a gallon, predicted the demise of the car. Cool. He and his buddies, all broke, went out to buy champagne to toast the good news. The car survived. Gas went to $2. More champagne and … then car owners started buying bikes to strap to their motors and take them out into the country for riding. But, DiNucci has survived, too. He came back to his independent roots and builds some of the most seductive machines around.

North American Handmade Bicycle Show 2010 Best Lugged Frame: A cherry-red lip-gloss glistening steel frame, olive green mudguards, stitched leather-bound handlebars with matching brake hood, large flange hubs,

single speed, a bike for fast coursing … *NAHBS 2011 Best of Show:* A townie with flat bars in the shape of a quizzical eyebrow, pale courgette smoothie frame with postbox red mudguards, gears and rear and front stay-mounted pencil beam lights, an apparent sylphlike lightness, to whisper through the unseen spaces in the muddle of urban sprawl.

The more bikes the better? You bet, he says. 'I'll tell you, what's going on in Portland is just beautiful and unbelievable. When I left making DiNucci bikes, no one else was really making bikes. And now all of a sudden, these things just blossomed and the kids are getting it. I don't know why it's taken most of my life for this to happen, but I'm glad it is. It's just beautiful.'

LEFT
DiNucci worked with Specialized from 1985 alongside Mike Sinyard. He designed the bikes in America and supervised their production in Japan. These days, he says, getting back to hands-on road bike crafting feels good.

Mount Washington, at the end of the road: DiNucci's patch of rural Oregon is so remote it might be at one of the imagined corners of the round earth.

A good fork is heavy: the cast crown needs to be rigid, straight and durable. DiNucci makes no apology for the weight.

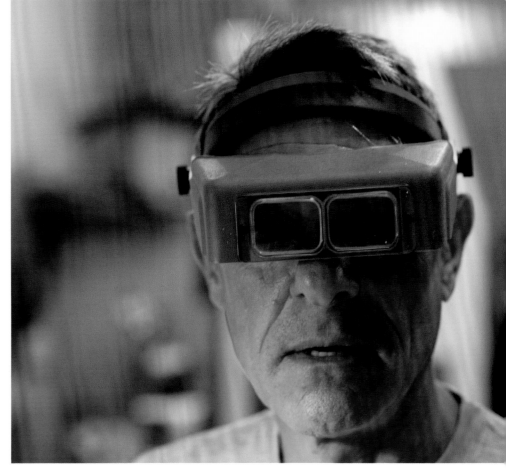

Magnifying glasses help Mark see any flaws in the frames. He is always his own sternest critic.

His new house and workshop now complete, Mark DiNucci gets down to some quality hand-finishing.

Almost forty years since starting out in the bike industry, Mark is back doing what he loves most. He credits Andy Newlands of Strawberry, along with his old VW van and a box of Columbus tubing, as early influences.

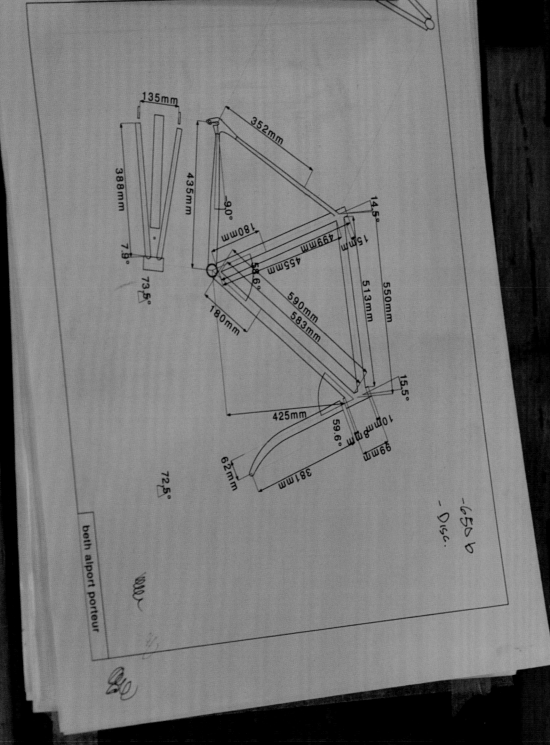

135mm

388mm

7.9°

73.5°

352mm

-9.0°

435mm

14.5°

180mm

15mm

499mm

455mm

58.6°

513mm

550mm

590mm

583mm

180mm

15.5°

425mm

59.6°

100mm

99mm

62mm

381mm

72.5°

650b

- Disc.

beth alport porteur

DIATECH®
BICYCLE COMPONENTS

IRA RYAN

The chrome badge on the head tube is a swallow, a bird proverbial for swift flight, harbinger of summer, bringer of luck to a house if it nests in the eaves. The Ira Ryan bike is an affirmation of its builder's free-ranging spirit, like the bird aloft in swift flight, in the soaring power of its propulsion, 'the achieve of, the mastery of the thing' as Gerard Manley Hopkins wrote of the Windhover, a falcon. In Ryan's own words: 'Epic is a 20-mile ride in the rain with three flats and lots of mud. Sometimes it's rain, gravel, climbing, or cookies and coffee in the middle of nowhere. Really it's as much about your state of mind as where you are and what you are doing. The rider makes the experience and the bike is just the ultimate accessory.'

Ryan has been building his elegant versions of *the ultimate accessory* in the basement of a bike shop in the St Johns neighbourhood, five miles north of Portland, Oregon, since 2005, after an apprenticeship at Vanilla Bicycles. His route to the craft of turning the best steel alloys from Columbus and Dedacciai, hand cut lugs, 56 per cent silver, into a frame with lots of time and care, was somewhat haphazard, albeit centred on a love of riding wherever, whenever. Tough conditions? Ideal. Bad weather, long distances, challenging road surfaces? Bring 'em on. Hardships and adversity, he says, promote our instinct to persevere and to subvert the creeping twofold menace of comfort and complacency. You relax, you let slip your energies. Stay bright, stay alert, keep sharp. As Voltaire put it: 'Work distances us from three great ills: boredom, vice and want.'

Ryan speaks enthusiastically of the transformative experience which riding a bike in extreme conditions can bring: 'Rolling into the darkness on never ending rolling hills and back roads covered in gravel with 180 miles down and another 130 to go … having just dropped the main

field, in the lead now and on target to win the first Trans Iowa, or Tranny … riding with my friend Ricky up Lolo Pass in the spring to find gravel and ice on the descent into Hood River. It was our first time riding all the way there from Portland. We stopped in Hood River to eat McDonalds before turning around and motor pacing 18-wheelers and traffic on I-84 the whole way home, just barely beating sunset. I think it was 130 miles total. Or it might be a group ride in Iowa with a tornado behind us, pace lining at 43mph with a killer, literally, fucking tailwind chasing us the whole way … riding 750-miles from San Francisco to Portland in four days, sleeping in a ditch four hours a night, as part of a Raid Race. Hell, even riding Saltzman [a 24 mile off-road circuit round Portland] is a favourite.'

As to what led him to full-time hand-crafting of frames, he did the bumming around thing: working in restaurants, washing dishes, cutting vegetables, general dogsbody … a carpenter … founder member of the Magpie Messenger Service, a Portland, Oregon courier collective, but he's been working on bikes since he was 17, both on his own bikes and as a shop mechanic, before the advent of Ira Ryan Cycles.

He's an unapologetic fan of lugged steel frames, down-tube shifters 'and riding without a helmet, but that's just me. If a carbon bike works for you, grab your 10-speed ride and let's go suffer some cobbles together'. The rough stuff and the precision work at the bench seem to meld in him, he lives and breathes the bike itself and the joy – and suffering – it can deliver. The 21-pound steel race machine was the bike he started on, a bike you can ride hard and put away wet – end of a race, fling it in the truck, never mind about paintwork or carbon forks fracturing. Does the fragility of carbon equate with a feebler mindset? Could be, in Ryan's mind. 'The heroic hard-man mythology, the Europeans and their spring classics, continue to motivate me, though I think [the whole ethos and culture] is being diluted by plastic bits and flammable parts.' For him, the essence is simple and uncompromising: 'Riding a bike up one side of a mountain and down the other on a bike that I made with my own two hands – using nothing but simple tools, fire and metal tubes – is my greatest achievement. I love that my craft hasn't changed much in generations. What I'm doing and the way I'm doing it is the same way my grandfather, had he made bikes, would have done things. That feels good. It feels solid. I think the best tool in the shop is the builder's hands. I think relying too heavily on technology to support your design and technique is risky. Quality is elusive, everywhere you look and in so many aspects of our daily lives, and I think independent bicycle frame builders are doing something small to change that.' Technology, he says, is dope. And, as more and more professional riders are beginning to say, and openly, Why would you dope?

Working to a plan. Every bike is different, each will fit its owner uniquely. The builder's hands, 'the best tools in the box' are only as good as the builder's mind.

Sweating the details and working his magic. Simple tools but expertly applied. Tubes are profiled and cut to perfection.

BELOW
Engineering in miniature. A porteur for the windowsill.

ABOVE
Classics races and classics riders are strong influences and in keeping with this, Ira believes a bicycle should feature reliability and all day comfort.

LEFT
Fillet brazed, bi-laminated or lugged. Ira says that a road bike should be sleek, graceful, precise and fast.

ABOVE
The Ryan workshop is right next to the house. Ira
has no excuse for extending his daily commute.

LEFT
Heat source and a filler rod. Brazing in action.

Recognition. Probably not the motivating factor but it must help.

Before: a bottom bracket shell tacked together.

After: a fillet brazed bottom bracket shell ready for the emery paper.

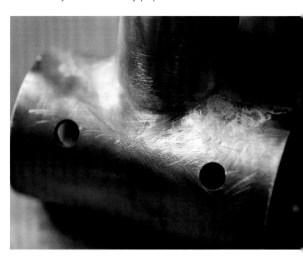

Every nook and cranny is filled with memorabilia, ephemera and in this case a clock.

FRAMES • Portland, Oregon, USA

TONY PEREIRA

Tony Pereira is a builder based in Portland, Oregon, where he lives but a stone's throw from his good friend and fellow frame-builder Ira Ryan. Pereira's *palmares* includes bikes in almost every genre from traditional super-skinny sleek road bikes through to big and beefy trail-taming 29"ers. Much like Ira though, Tony loves to build practical bikes, useful machinery to be ridden daily to and from work whatever the weather, and Portland has plenty of weather. Many of them feature racks and fenders (mudguards to the European) and somewhere sensible to stow a U-lock and there are neat accessories available such as a machined aluminium fender mounted taillight.

This closeness both in terms of approach and geography led to the creation of Breadwinner Cycles in 2013, a joint venture between Ryan and Pereira. The new company will offer a range of TIG welded custom steel bikes built by hand in Portland with the best of US-made components. Both of the signature builders will continue to build under their own names however but Breadwinner will offer something a little less expensive, produced a little more quickly.

The United Bicycle Institute, also in Portland, is world famous. It was founded more than thirty years ago with the aim of making learning about bicycles fun. The two campuses are well equipped and students come to soak up valuable two-wheeled knowledge, either to further their careers within the industry or simply to gain a better understanding of what they are riding. Courses are available in many aspects of bicycle matters but it is the frame-building department that we visited to witness Tony giving a class in the theory and practice of brazing steel. He's a popular lecturer and a good teacher. As he talks it becomes clear that brazing is one of the things Tony loves to do best and while this is a basic class the students see the theory of lugs and fillets become reality.

LEFT
Framebuilding is often described as an art but its also a craft but probably more importantly it's an engineering discipline. Steel tubes are very thin and light, when they're joined as a bicycle frame they're expected to be very strong.

RIGHT
As well as being an outstanding build in his own right Tony Pereira works as a guest lecturer at the United Bicycle Institute in Portland to pass on his experience.

LEFT
In his home workshop Tony creates bicycles and components for the road, the street and the mountain. Portland is a town with a rich and mixed cycling culture. Like most Portland folk he's more bothered with the fact that you are riding, than what you're riding.

ABOVE
Simple techniques like the correct use of a saw can make a huge difference to the way that tubes fit together before they are assembled, by keeping gaps to a minimum.

ABOVE
The facility at the United Bicycle Institute in Portland gives Tony the opportunity to pass on best practice and inspire the next generation.

They're given advice on cutting the metal to size, making sure the saw blade is sharp. On using a file, the right file for the job. Sitting the two pieces to be joined together to check the fit then making another adjustment if required. He insists that only when you are completely happy with the dry joint should you light up the torch.

The exercise for the morning session is to fix a dummy dropout into a piece of chainstay with the slot that they have just cut. Tony goes first and talks the class through the process from clamping into a vice through to applying the flux, directing the heat into the thicker metal (the dropout) and placing the filler rod. He wants them to use gravity and capillary action to flow the solder deep into the socket so as to fully support the dropout. Once he's finished his piece of work he lets it cool whilst taking and giving questions and answers.

Then there's the moment of truth. Tony takes another saw and neatly dissects the joint he's just made. We all crane forwards to see a perfect, shiny neat nugget of brass wrapped around the blue grey steel. Thus inspired, the students set to work at their own benches. They're well on the way to producing their own high-quality road or mountain bike frame as promised to them in the course prospectus.

RIGHT
Once the joint has been formed and given time to cool then Tony calls the students to watch as he cuts it into two pieces. Proof, if any was needed, that the joint is good.

Students gather round Tony as he explains the principles of heat transfer through the joint. Keeping the flame moving so as not to damage the tubing but also allow the solder to do its job.

FRAMES • Springfield, Oregon, USA

'When I see an adult on a bicycle, I do not despair for the future of the human race.'
H.G. Wells

WINTER

I write this shortly after the eleventh hour of the eleventh day of the eleventh month when, in 1918, the Armistice of the Great War began and the guns along the Western Front fell silent. Since I have referred here and there in this book to the link between the bicycle as a peaceable invention and the beating of ploughshares from swords, perpetual image of the quieting of mankind's belligerent impulse, it seems appropriate to begin this account of the work of Eric Estlund at Winter Cycles in Oregon, with his own contribution to the centenary of the start of that terrible conflict: The Winter Bicycles '1918'. An eccentricity, for sure, but a quirk of entirely potent charm and compassionate deliberation on man's inhumanity to man.

Unlike a number of the combatant armies which fought in the 1914–18 War, the US Army did not have a designated bicycle corps for front line troops. However, some 30,000 military bicycles were paid for by the US government to supply various uses in their Signal Corps, Intelligence section, as well as in Despatch, Liaison and personal transport. The model used, the Columbia Military, was chosen for its 'sturdiness of construction and utter trustworthiness' and it is the Columbia's pattern which Estlund has recreated – double bar top tube (originally to cope with the shocking roads of northern France), seamless tubes, Sturmey Archer hub gear, the machine and matching mudguards painted in the olive drab of the US forces, with a matte finish. Modern materials would make the double bar redundant but authenticity counts and, as one commentator remarks, 'they look killer'. Estlund has added a sweet nostalgic touch: on either side of the head tube, in the fork crowns, he has placed two pennies, cent coins, one dated 1914, the other 1918.

Brazing into a lug or a fork crown ...

Let Estlund, the very image of a West Coast hippy, Schubert glasses, ear rings, full beard and body-paint tattooed forearms, introduce himself:

'I am the designer, builder, email guy and official floor sweeper here at Winter. I have worked and played in many areas of the cycling world. I recognised early on the freedom and excitement of riding, not just competitively but also recreationally. It became part of how I chose to explore my world. In my college years I started working as a bicycle advocate to help bring more people and bicycles together. I have led both road and off-road tours for children and adults and continued to work as an advocate and teacher to promote safe, community minded sport and commuter cycling. Along the way I picked up an art degree with a focus on metal sculpture and function as well as 14 years of experiential based outdoor, art and environmental teaching experience. I have worked in fitting, retail and rental sales and as a builder for a very busy custom bicycle manufacturer.

'What does all that mean for you? It means … I can work with you to help design your perfect daily driver city bike, your health conscious trainer or your specific event competition machine. I know how to listen, and my one goal is to put you on the best fitting and performing bicycle for your needs.'

Estlund's background in art comes to the fore in his shaping of elegant, shiny snout, old-style stems – rounded jaw at the end of the extension to make a collar grip round the bars – and forks. A friend came in a while back with a pair of cracked forks and asked Estlund to make an identical copy. It wasn't the first pair of crash damaged forks the man had brought in – unlucky, or what? Now, this triggers recall of one of cycling history's epic moments of tenacity and sheer resource, namely when Eugène Christophe hefted his broken bike down the Col du Tourmalet to the village at the mountain's foot and fashioned replacement forks from pipes in a blacksmith's forge. Estlund didn't have commissaries docking time or penalising him for taking assistance from the boy at the forge, but his work did call for a specific ingenuity. As he describes it: 'The fork was a unicrown design with some

The headbadge motif represents a Chinese winter flowering plum tree, noted for its resistance to cold weather.

ABOVE
The pillar drill. Pretty much a workshop essential.

RIGHT
A fillet-brazed joint doesn't use a lug. The tubes are clamped together and then a fillet of brass is built up around the two tubes. It's difficult and time-consuming work but the end result looks superb.

Designer, metal sculptor and artist Eric Estlund has already built an enviable reputation as well as some very desirable frames. He makes around 25 to 35 complete custom bikes a year as well as a limited number of bikes for contract.

tall, non-standard measurements. To accommodate the extra crown height, as well as the lower relative brake position, I had to do a little sculptural reconstruction.' The result, a gleaming pair of blades, slim and highly polished, that might be the tuning fork for a perfect wheel, is evidence of the loving care of this craftsman. A neat coincidence that he lives in … Eugene, Oregon.

The first bike he built, a grass track frame, spare of form, lean in outline, beautifully proportioned, occasioned him the two most important reactions for a craftsman: pride and dissatisfaction. The one is the core of the desire, the other the spur to improve, always to improve. He built it under the tutelage of the people at the United Bicycle Institute where he learned 'a proven method to build a bike and [the first steps on] a proper path of self-education'. The best way to learn how to do something is to do it, and by his own reckoning, in his first year as a tyro brazer at UBI, he 'pushed about 380 pounds, 11 miles of brass over roughly 3000 bikes'.

Estlund is highly regarded, not only by the small coterie of custom builders in Oregon – he is Chairman of the Oregon Association of Bicycle Builders – but by his customers, precisely because he takes the whole notion of custom very seriously. A sadly depleted word, 'customer'. For people travelling by train? What happened to passenger? A customer is someone who customarily buys from a trader, a favourite shop or market stall, because they depend on the quality of the goods on sale. That's what Estlund sees and in the men and women who come to him, it's what he honours and cherishes. Thus, on a day, 'a few months ago, a local student approached me asking that I build my take on a classic 3Rensho track bike. He wanted to keep the frame as traditional as possible but with provision for brakes and a comfortable position for street use'. The result? Need you ask.

As well as classic lugs Eric also uses bi-lamination, a technique that nods at lugged and fillet brazed construction. A sleeve is joined to the end of a tube which, being thicker, gives as strong a joint as a lug but offers more options for angles and resembles both a fillet brazed joint and a lugged joint.

The horizontal dropouts here are a classy response to a world where the vertical has taken over.

SPÉCIALITÉS TA

'The thing about TA' the enthusiasts for the marque from early days will tell you, 'it's bombproof' and the Director, Mme Sylvie Breuil, grand-daughter of TA's founder, Georges Navet, has never seen a broken TA axle or chainring in all the time she's been involved, and only ever once a broken crank.

In the foyer of the TA premises in Sissonne, a blown-up black and white photograph of an elderly man and a young girl: Navet and his daughter, Mme Breuil's mother. TA offers the biggest range of chainrings available on the world market and it is chainrings on which they concentrate. Any size of ring which the narrow range of both Shimano and Campagnolo do not manufacture, TA will supply. Such diversity always was their great selling point and it remains so.

Georges Navet was a joiner/carpenter. He was also a man with an idea. In the course of his work at the bench, he pondered the question: why not a front-wheel drive mechanism for the bicycle? He was prompted by the recent invention (in the 1930s) of a front-wheel drive car by Citroën, following Audi and Adler. Perhaps, too, his thoughts ran on the aluminium used by Citroën for their TPV (*tout petite voiture*), precursor of the famous 2CV which hit, or, rather, lightly scuffed, the road in 1948. Sadly for Navet, his *traction avant* didn't work. But, in the course of his experiments, his subconscious mind stayed on the *qui vive* and the one failed dream spawned a tangential thought of sweet brilliance: the aluminium chainwheel of widely varying size. The father of the Tour de France, Henri Desgrange, had outlawed the use of

Since 1947 machines like this have been used to produce the highest quality components, although today computerised (CNC) plant is more common.

An Austrian supplier works closely with TA to give them the necessary quality raw material

ABOVE
It's fortunate that aluminium is a very easy material to recycle.

RIGHT
Soft aluminium needs to be turned very quickly compared to steel but the bit must advance slowly and in small increments to avoid gouging.

TOP LEFT
'Poinçonnage' means punching but there's also a lot of milling, machining and turning in transforming a sheet of aluminium into a chainwheel.

ABOVE
Anodising involves immersion in an electrolyte bath, through which passes an electric current along a cathode. The aluminium component becomes the anode which results in a process of controlled oxidisation.

LEFT
Anodising gives a bright, shiny surface that looks good, is easy to clean, and resists wear.

the new-fangled derailleur gear because it gave unfair advantage and was unreliable, to boot. He died in 1939; the development and improvement of the fairly crude gear mechanism proceeded and, in the first post-War Tour, riders were using derailleur gears, double chainwheels and changers.

Aluminium, the third most abundant element, after oxygen and silicon, is soft, durable, lightweight, ductile and malleable, i.e. easily worked. It's highly resistant to corrosion, non-magnetic and does not produce sparks. Pure aluminium is quite weak but, when mixed in alloy with other metals, becomes astonishingly strong. It's also remarkably versatile, readily machined, cast, drawn and extruded.

Cyclotourisme had a big following in France before the War. After it, when petrol was so scarce and heavily rationed, the bike became even more popular and Navet realised that enthusiasts across a whole range of strengths and abilities needed gear ratios that would help them explore France's multifarious terrain. Everything came together: aluminium alloy, multiple sizes of chainwheel, his own expertise. Crank arms followed.

Perhaps with a whimsical nod at his earlier failure, Navet called his operation TA and, within a very few years, from a workshop in Meudon, then in nearby Clamart, he was producing chain rings for tourists but also for racing men. And it was the racing men who gave his new enterprise vital publicity. Tour winners, Coppi … Robic … Bartali … Bobet … Gaul … all riding on TA chainwheels. Navet's fertile imagination, meanwhile, had dreamed up the retractable hard plastic nipple, the *obturateur*, on the bidon which made taking a swig whilst in full motion much easier. From 1948, TA bidons supplied the Tour de France and did so for the next forty years. From the very beginning, in order to accommodate the needs of their core customers who asked for the outlandish ratios which the big manufacturers did not make, TA produced the fit-all spider crank and the independently fixed rings. Thus, any combination of chainwheels could be assembled or replaced. It is the basis on which the company operates still. Customers demand, they supply and the time between order and delivery is rarely longer than two weeks, routinely quicker because, of the seven hundred different products they make, most are always in stock. Moreover, every chainwheel they produce is compatible with every other system on the market, contrasted with the reclusive nature of Shimano, for example, whose chain rings are difficult to get and the company itself niggardly in its jealous refusal to adapt to any other make.

The company was transformed by Mme Breuil's father, a primary school teacher, who, one day, told his father-in-law Georges that he felt sure he could make a better machine for producing crank arms. And he did. His

And in many cases there is more choice, for example, rings which increase in one tooth increments.

daughter explains: 'He and my grandfather got on very well and I suppose he'd been thinking about improving the process. And that's what he did.'

She says this with such aplomb, such casual acceptance, one may conclude that shafts of inventive brilliance are run-of-the-mill in the family, that technological aperçus arrive with satisfying regularity. However, asked 'But where did that come from?', she does that classic French thing: she shrugs her shoulders and, again, smiles.

TA chainrings are delicate, finely machined, elegant, objects which some people, not so fancifully, either, compare to jewellery, slender, pin-bright, as if tooled by elves.

On one wall of the conference room a poster puffing their cranks and chain rings tells us: '*Un symbole … Etre un symbole ça se batit, ça se mérite, c'est vous donner satisfaction*'. To be a symbol, you have to build it, to deserve it,

it's satisfying. (Implied: it takes time.) Elsewhere: 'The quality of the aluminium is the quality of the product'.

The matter of quality is simple: TA have to provide only the very best that metallurgy and machinery can make. That's doctrinal. The competition is so very fierce that any lapse in standards, inimical as it is to the TA ethic, would be unthinkable. They've been using an aluminium-magnesium alloy for ten years, working in close cooperation with a foundry in Austria, one of only two in Europe to deal with similar requirements. The crucial task is to eliminate any contaminating material. They also collaborate with engineers from Audi, who visit the Sissonne plant for discussion. Audi, a huge company, can spend much more time on research and development than TA but they share ideas and the two Sissonne r&d men are experts in their field. The collaboration serves both enterprises, the goal is shared, the ideas pooled and both sides gain, a timely example of European teamwork for a global market.

For a chainring, the teeth must be precisely cut so that they mesh perfectly with the (steel) chain over many thousands of revolutions.
They must also have the necessary ramps and profiles to pick up the chain and drop it smoothly again.

SPOKES • Antwerp, Belgium

Stamping out the CX X Ray with a force of 400 tonnes, to smash the single piece of wire into shape, a shock so powerful that the ground around the machine shakes.

'Life is like riding a bicycle. To keep your balance, you must keep moving.'
Albert Einstein.

SAPIM

We all remember, don't we, the moment when the wheels beneath us ran true for the first time and we were riding a bicycle. We are, for ever after, in thrall to gyroscopic motion. And so, the wheel, the magical filigree of structure, the mystery of its strength in lightness. To move the wheel forward and rotate, it needs energy, the energy transmitted by the rider through the hubs. The heavier the wheel, the more energy it requires and stores, the harder it is to stop. That stored energy goes to waste when the brakes are applied. Ergo the lighter the wheel, that compound of some seventy-four individual parts, the faster it will roll.

Solid wooden wheel, heavy, a bright spark thinks. Cut down the quantity of wood, spokes are born. Spoked bicycle wheels arrived, thanks to the genius of James Starley and William Hillman, in 1870. In 1874, the breakthrough: Starley invented tangent spoking. By placing spokes at a tangential angle to the hub (as opposed to radially, straight out of the hub to the rim), the force delivered to the hub by the action of pedalling pulls directly in line with the spokes and the spokes pull on the rim – with a motion similar to stroking a hoop along with a stick – so that hub and rim may accelerate and decelerate in concert and without twisting. The torsional rigidity of the wheel may be further enhanced by different patterns of crossing the spokes, lacing them over and under adjacent spokes, in a sort of open weave. As the wheel moves, the spokes flex which makes for a very smooth ride.

A word, too, on the way spokes work. A solid wheel acts by compression, transferring the weight of the rider directly to the ground. A spoke-formed wheel works through tension. The weight is not supported by the spokes beneath the hub, but suspended from the

167

Straight from the drum the stainless wire would not be true enough for a spoke so it first has to be teased into submission along a series of rollers, cutters and straighteners. Quality control is an obsession.

ABOVE
Cutting threads, by hand, one by one. Each thread,
after suitable preparation, to join with the nipple.

LEFT
Drawing the wire to the correct diameter.

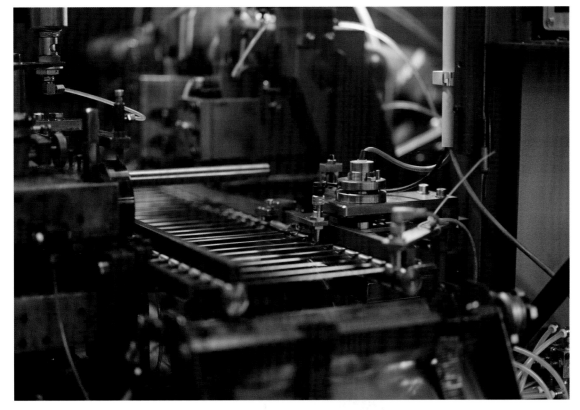

upper rim. Indeed, a stationary bicycle can be held in position by wheels threaded with a mere two spokes. The rim will lose its circular shape in such circumstances but the illustration is made. Add more spokes and the rim retains its round form.

And so, the time has come to talk of spokes. For the first lightweight pair of wheels a friend built for me, I bought a quiver of spokes such as might have been teased from a seam of goblin silver, worked to airy thinness by elvin smiths in a subterranean cavern lit by inextinguishable crystal and given their final glint by diamond polishers in Antwerp. And, to Antwerp we go, to the hub of SAPIM, elite spoke makers.

It begins with a drum of coil wire from various sources, all to SAPIM's precise specification, from which are taken samples for testing in their in-house laboratory. The wire is subjected to tests for plasticity and elasticity – can it

be shaped and stretched to the level required? Indeed, they are extended to breaking point in an elongation jig. It's a fierce interrogation and, if the wire is not fit, the manufacturer has to pay for the shipment. The failure of a spoke may mean the collapse of a wheel and who knows what damage to the rider? You know the old saw: For want of a nail, the kingdom was lost … (Lost nail, cast horseshoe, king toppled off and killed.)

Two SAPIM plants (there's another in France) produce some 600,000 spokes, of 18/8 stainless steel (i.e. with 18 per cent chromium, 8 per cent nickel) or zinc, of different grades, profiles, refinement, coupled with one or other of around 500 different configurations of brass or aluminium nipples. They can customise spokes for different hubs, according to request from wheel makers – to accommodate different sizes and shapings of hubs and rims. Their Polyax profile for the head of the nipple is a notable improvement on traditional form and, needless to say, the efficiency of the juncture of

Spokes work in tension for the most part but must also resist compression as well as the torque of lateral loads caused by cornering, braking and accelerating.

A good wheel is a close-knit, equal partnership of hub, rim and spokes, a trinity wherein the spoke is rarely considered.

Single butted, double butted or profiled: Sapim make them all.

nipple and spoke contributes to the reliability of the wheel. Why do they not use steel for the nipple? Because steel against steel will not turn as well as brass which has a naturally oily character. A brass nipple will still turn years after it's been fitted, whereas an aluminium nipple will tend to harden. SAPIM, to the surprise of some experts in the arcana of spokes, insist that their aluminium nipples which undergo a pre-lubrication and surface treatment are stronger than the brass. They will not, however, say a word about their butting process – the secret method by which the ends of the spoke are thickened, for strength, by swaging or extrusion. For, even in the apparently limited world of spoke manufacture, industrial espionage is a danger.

The SAPIM technical men explain certain aspects of the manufacturing process: the two-stage cutting of the butted bars, pre-cut and fine, all waste collected as scrap for reuse … the forge die for pressing the head into form

and to reduce the burring of the metal to a minimum … a complex variety of bending adjusted to hub and wheel diameter, a process wherein the wheel builder can make calamitous errors which compromise endurance and strength … a searching investigation into the technology of their aluminium nipples to ensure an item which is light, strong, low friction, colourful and easy to mount …

Their current top-range CX-Ray spoke (made from Fagesta wire produced in Sweden) has an oval section and the manner of their making gives some apology for the high price of the item. Each spoke goes through a massive press which applies 400 tonnes to the wire to form the profile. There are two such presses and from them issue 7000 spokes per 24-hour day. Question not the cost, then, of the glittering spoke in your wheel, compressed by these giants and given their especial gloss in old Antwerp.

Their Polyax profile for the head of the nipple is a notable improvement on traditional form... steel against steel will not turn as well as brass.

Stainless wire works its way along the production line prior to cutting. There are many spoke lengths available and are determined by the hub-rim combination.

HUBS • Portland, Oregon, USA

Headsets and hubs. Two components which have
made the King name since 1976.

'Next he came to the centre of all creation, (the *hub* they
call it there) …'
Charles Kingsley, *The Water Babies*

CHRIS KING

The pivot, the holding pin, the axis round which it all turns, universe, idea, movement, wheel.
Chris King introduced his hub to the general picture circa 1976. Toughest and lightest, that's
the claim, and it would be a bold cynic to gainsay it. Certainly they look very fine and they are
very fine.

At the heart of the hub is the bearing. The history of the load-bearing ball is long – ancient
Egyptians, Roman engineers, Leonardo da Vinci, of course (in a design for a helicopter, what
else?), Galileo, the famous horologist John Harrison, and, in 1794, when the French were
well into their own programme of another sort of revolutionary motion, the Welshman Philip
Vaughan. Of his own bearings, King writes:

'Inside the hubshells, the business transaction of putting your power to work, is where you'll
find what matters most … it's our bearings, axles and engagement system that have earned
the trust of discerning cyclists. We make our own bearings in-house, each hand-checked for
precision and built with a robust sealing system. Best of all? [You can] service them yourself.
Our strong, constant diameter axles run through the bearings to the frame and fork dropouts
for precise handling and stiffness under power.'

He then gets technical which, naturally, he must, and the detail, the minute detail, of
conception and construction, is what makes the hubs so prized. 'Every King rear hub is
powered by Chris's patented RingDrive™ engagement system. This unique design offers

RIGHT
The King production line is secretive. Only approved photography is ever seen so as not to give up any secrets.

BELOW
Assembly is skilled work and King have developed their own tools for use on the production line and in the workshop.

The tubing and billets needed for the Cielo bikes and the hub/headsets come exclusively from North American mills with carefully 'verified' manufacturing processes.

As befits a bicycle company, King take recycling very seriously. Although they get through a lot of metal and oil, they make sure that they don't waste anything. Swarf and offcuts are collected and compacted into a 'puck' while the soy-based machine oil is drained, cleaned and reused.

Chris King. The face and brand of the company.

CNC machining, precision lathe work and accurate cutting transform base metal into the headsets, hubs and bottom brackets we all admire.

instant, positive engagement that is over three times quicker than a standard 24-tooth pawl-type free hub. RingDrive™ uses 72 engagement teeth on stainless steel drive and driven rings for a system that is capable of handling torque load of over 800 ft/lbs. Our R45 road racing hub has its own 45-tooth stainless steel RingDrive™ for further reduced drag and noise.' Quiet as a movement of air over glass.

There is the colour range, too – silver, pewter, gold, mango, red, navy, green, brown, black, pink …
Pink?

Child psychologists have determined, from observation, that the two colours infants most dislike are brown and … pink. Yikes. Where does that leave Barbie? But wait. The King pink is part of the company's wider remit. They not only recycle aluminium shavings for reuse, they champion the bike as 'a tool to encourage and inspire'. The Pretty and Strong pink hub and headsets exist to help to raise awareness of research into breast cancer. They even encourage their customers to replace a ride with time out to urge a female friend to take a mammogram and part of the sale of any Pretty and Strong component is donated to cancer research. As to the recycling, after two seconds of 400-ton hydraulic force, a small pile of alu chips – the metal waste produced when a component piece is formed on a machine

– come out as pucks. About 98 per cent of the waste oil squeezed out of the compressed chips is filtered, clarified and sent back to lubricate the machines. Both metal and oil saved from waste.

It's stimulating to note, too, that they are articulate in their assessment of the differing demands of a hub. There are probably people, evoking the spirit of Gertrude Stein, who would say a hub is a hub is a hub. Not so. Compare and contrast the cyclo-cross bike with the road machine. The latter – up to six hours continuous stress on roads that go up down and around, with intermittent injections of severe acceleration. The former – an hour of unremitting pace, the drag of mud, snag of vegetation, jag of violent switches of direction, frenetic braking, shuddering jumps and drops, followed by the savage attentions of a water cannon (hose) to clean the whole caboodle. Punishment of an entirely singular type. But, then, the American enthusiasm for cycling began with, is rooted in, rough-country riding. 'Cyclo-cross is a passion here in the Northwest', says King. 'We pour coffee every Sunday at the renowned Cross Crusade Race Series for hardened racers and rain-soaked spectators. And we love it. For these people we developed the all-new Classic Cross hubset.'

And here, another and delightful element in the King outreach: The Gourmet Century. Only sensible reaction? Wow.

LEFT

A Chris King component is a fit and forget kind of purchase because the owner continues to appreciate the quality and performance long after the price has been forgotten.

ABOVE

Ready for a close up, one of the inspection bays in the workshop. Chris King quality control is phenomenal.

TOP RIGHT

Much of the tooling is made especially for the King production line.

RIGHT

Bearings ready for assembly. The humble egg box proving useful as a holding bay.

July: the north-westerly pastoral hinterland of Portland, Oregon, farms and barns, vineyards and fields, a single track wooden railway bridge, sans parapet, tree-shaded stretches of loose-stoned bridle-path winding across the arable land, small town Oregon, colonial-style clapperboard houses and churches along the way. The Gourmet Century – 60 non-competitive miles for 'rabbits and meandering sightseers alike' – is the signature event of the Chris King Precision Components event calendar. The 2012 theme, Farm Fresh, celebrated the cuisine and culture of local farmers with the support of a group of renowned blue riband restaurateurs preparing delectable treats served at three strategically spaced epicurean rest points to keep the 'appetite piqued and the legs energized'. One might question the legs energised … more likely the morale, but a glance at the menu would have

you saying 100k? Nah, easy-peasy, bring on the catering.

Hearty breakfast at Chris King's headquarters, tasty treats en route, a sumptuous gussied-up (Sunday best) picnic lunch, and back to the factory, Chris King himself plying the chef's *batterie de cuisine* in the company's top-of-the-range chow house, for a full table service, sit-down banquet. Green bean salad with hazelnut and goat's cheese dressing … cold cucumber and dill soup … braised emmer wheat with scallions, pickled fruit and ricotta salad … spit-roasted hog, fresh shell beans, peppers and salmoriglio sauce … flourless chocolate cake with local berries and a tart raspberry sauce. Dinner concludes, not with speeches but with a sneak peek into the making of Chris King Precision Components. Wow.

LEFT
Billets, rods, tubes and blocks of raw and mostly heavy materials have to be cut into manageable sizes before they're taken to the shop floor.

ABOVE
King also manufacture Cielo frames and bicycles in a small annexe within the main factory. They're not strictly a custom builder but it is a high quality outfit with a dedicated team of cutters, braziers and painters. (The Camino Cielo, the Sky's Pathway, is a road in the Santa Ynez Mountains near Santa Barbara.)

Innovative and independent, Cliff Polton (the man who designed the toilet flush handle on Concorde) likes to push the boundaries of conventional thinking in his designs.

ROYCE

Asked why the company is called Royce, the founder and chief engineer, Cliff Polton, says that the name has a ring of quality to it – a nod to Henry Royce, partner of Charles Rolls, the genius duo behind the Rolls-Royce automotive legend. Polton himself is an aficionado of the pedal car (of which more later) which may be no more than a sort of highly sophisticated joke at the expense of the internal combustion engine. His principal working obsession is with bicycle hubs and bottom brackets. Precision engineered to a refinement which has evoked comparisons between the Royce component and jewelled *objets* such as might have graced the dressing table of a Tsarina of all the Russias. There is no secret in the way Royce achieves such ultra closeness of specification: they use only the very best bearings available and then subject them to further test and polishing which eliminates even the suggestion of that whimsical element in high-end engineering – tolerance, slippage. It may have been said before, it bears saying again: Polton does regard his hubs on a par with works of art. As Alexander Pope puts it: 'What oft was thought but ne'er so well express'd.' It takes work, vision, insistence on the best and there is no such thing tolerable as second best. There must be no trace of machining marks left. The only final surface coating he accepts are silver anodising or gold Ti nitride plating beneath which no flaws can be hidden.

Royce use only titanium and aluminium, in whatever proportion best suits the need for durability and stiffness. A hub must run true else it is not rightly a hub and if Polton has a distinctly eccentric manner of speaking about his right hubs, then that may only be his way of letting off creative steam in the process of such crucial application of the sternest of high standards in the making them. He does employ a carbon sleeve between the flanges in one special hub – the racing gold hub – but that is the only hint of black in the parts

Cliff isn't a man for patents and paperwork and claims that he'd be flattered if one of his designs were to be copied. This hub lubricating system is definitely one of his better ideas.

fashioned in the cluttered workshop a short way inland from the waters of the Solent, west of what used to be the ever-turning hub of the British Navy, Portsmouth. Why no black? He does not like black. A nice counter, even late in the day, to Henry 'any colour so long as it's black' Ford, originator of assembly line cars.

There is no hint of such roll-on roll-off thinking in the Royce set-up. Innovation, restless searching for improvement, the drive to improve and perfect is central, at the hub, so to say. Polton has the fidgety, curious, 'what-if?' mind and intelligence of a superior inventor. As example, the track cranks he came up with in London's Olympic year. The Tri-lobe bottom bracket, a complicated shape – tapered spindle in triangular form – of whose efficiency Polton is utterly convinced. Tri refers to 'torsional rigidity', offering equal contact down its length. Of the origin of, inspiration for, the shape he is sardonically evasive, speaking airily about Wimbledon Technical

College, the Germans, 1937 truck drive shafts ... shafts which may be no more than his way of saying even he can't be absolutely sure, now. Why, then, had no one hit on the idea before? A mystery, but that is the thing about revolutionary ideas – in this case the ultimate, purely revolutionary idea, surely – they don't get thought of that easily, albeit they seem so crazily simple once someone has boldly conceived of and then enunciated the principle. Add to that Polton's dictum that 'nothing is perfect ... it can always be improved upon' and the route to startling principles of manufacture is laid out. It just takes a bit of search and the lamplike glare of a radiant sensibility to technical problems and solutions. Further, Polton concentrates on his own ways and means. He never looks over anyone else's shoulder. That way lies distraction. There is no consummation in mimicry. When challenged about his way and that of the big beasts, Shimano and Campagnolo, he eschews comparison, raises a whimsical eyebrow at copying. Why, he even personally designed the flush handles of the loos on board Concorde. And

The team at Royce is small, the production runs are limited but the quality is legendary.

185

he doesn't even patent his breakthroughs. This apparent commercial disdain is no such thing but points to a loftier, an essential, belief in human ingenuity and a modest sense that he is doing no more than contribute to its works. If he has a great idea and everyone uses it then … reason to be cheerful. As the great Greek historian Thucydides said of his magisterial, ground-breaking work, he intended it as 'a possession for all time' – *ktëma es aei*.

The entrance corridor to the Royce works bruits the talent its hubs have helped to ever quicker speed – like treasured messages on a kitchen cork board, the walls dotted with posters, cards and framed cuttings from Nicole Cooke, Glen Longland, Chris Boardman, Ian Cammish … Polton has backed Cooke for years since her junior days and she still keeps in touch. The week before the London 2012 Olympic road race she dropped in midway through a training ride to say hello. Chris Boardman, the high priest of mechanical nicety, came to Royce for his hubs. Sean Yates, a man prone to forget to take his shoes to a time-trial, knew to come to Royce for what he *couldn't* leave behind.

Polton relaxes by driving pedal cars. Yes. Now, I recall pedal cars from the infant nursery in whose playground I cruised, wee boy racer, and can't make anything like a match between them and the sort of gem-like bits and pieces Polton concentrates his mind on perfecting. However, there obviously is some connexion. Maybe I was simply not driving the right kind of pedal car, the hi-spec, Grand Prix HPV (oh, come on, keep up: Human-Powered Vehicle), up to a big one of anybody's money (please, *do* concentrate: a thousand smackers). Cool.

Setting up the machining for the Trilobe bottom bracket was challenging but getting that mirror-like finish on the crank arms isn't easy either.

Shiny, hard and long lasting, a fusion of carbon fibre and gold nitride is also expensive to manufacture and to buy.

TOP LEFT
Cutting, milling, drilling and turning are central to the Royce factory. Titanium and aluminium both submit to the bite of hardened tool steel.

ABOVE
A Royce QR skewer has quality and precision running through its DNA.

LEFT
Hub shells ready for assembly with bearings and axles.

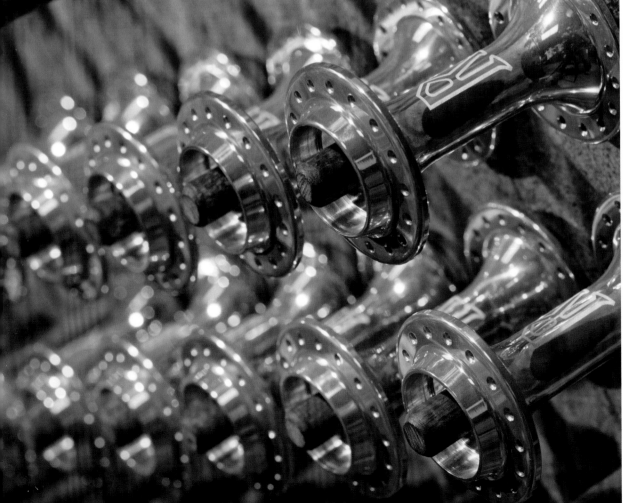

Flagship wheels. The SSC Cosmic Carbon. They look
fast standing still. Constant refinement and working
alongside pro teams pushes the design envelope
every year.

MAVIC

One day in 1889, a memorable date for a revolution, two brothers, Léon and Laurent Vielle,
set up a nickel-plating business in Lyon, France, with Henry Gormand as president. Shortly
afterwards, two friends, Charles Idoux and Lucien Chanel, also sponsored by Gormand,
launched another enterprise for 'the fabrication and sale of spare parts for bicycles'. They
called their business *Manufacture d'Articles Vélocipédiques Idoux et Chanel*. Mavic was born.
At the time, there were an estimated 203,000 bicycles in France; by 1914, some 3.5 million.
The popular craze for cycling, which gave workers their own transport at an affordable price,
was also fuelled by a fanatical enthusiasm for bike races. The first modern Olympic Games
in 1896 included a road race, reflecting the wider trend for major professional long-distance
road races which not only fired the popular imagination but served as publicity for the reliability
of the innovative two-wheeled machine. It is for wheels that Mavic is, and was from the start,
best known.

To accommodate the ill-surfaced roads of the early years, the basic components of any
bicycle, wheels and frame, needed to be robust and, to a degree, flexible, sturdy enough
to endure the shocking onslaught on man and bike imposed by (for example) the Tour de
France, first run in 1903, but resilient, too, to absorb the rough nature of the roads.

The Vielle and Mavic operations soon combined under the Mavic name and, by 1925, when
the firm relocated in Lyon, they had added mudguards and steel rims to their manufacturing
line. They also produced handlebars, and, between 1909 and 1933, the evolution of their

The long, flat rim extrusions in the state that they arrive into the warehouse. All manner of machining and milling await.

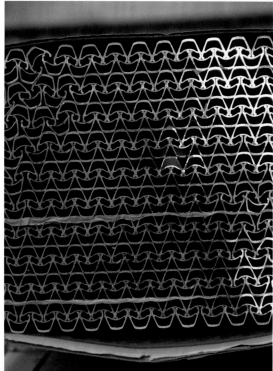

From the straight extrusion to the basic hoop these rims-to-be await their joint and then onto the machining.

A great deal of technology is hidden within the rim. You might not even know it is there but you would probably notice its absence.

The angle of the spoke holes and the width of the spoke holes is a vital part of keeping the wheel strong and true. They must match with the nipple precisely and be snug enough so as not allow any unnecessary play.

Some of the Mavic machines are strictly off limits to cameras. Specialist robots have been designed by the in-house engineers to do a very specific job and, proud as they are of the end result, Mavic sometimes won't let on how they've achieved it.

bars, made of Duralumin, was in constant development. The Mavic bars supplied the demand of a swelling number of cyclo-touring customers, amateur riders keen to explore the wider reaches of the continent, mountains especially, in the wake of the Great Bike Race. It was an essential part of the Mavic appeal and ethos that they catered to all cyclists with equal fidelity to their needs.

Duralumin (literally 'hard earth of alum'), an alloy of aluminum with small amounts of copper and manganese, was invented by the German metallurgist Alfred Wilm in 1903. Hard and resistant to tearing, it was much used in the early aviation industry – for the corrugated skinning of the Junkers aircraft in WWI, the internal frames of Zeppelins … In the early 1930s, Mavic produced a rim made of duralumin which featured an eyelet whose edges spread out in a lip over the top and lower surfaces of the hollow rim, better to carry the stress of the spokes. (The spokes give a wheel its bouncing quotient.) Mavic named one model of handlebars after the independent professional, Benoît-Faure, twice winner of the *touriste-routier* category of the Tour de France, and Mavic's links with professional riders were, unsurprisingly, always vital to their early advertising. The French rider Antonin Magne, winner of the 1931 Tour, tested the Dura rims in the 1934 race, but secretly. Rules stipulated the use of wooden rims so the Mavic rims, weighing 750gms, were painted to look like wood. Magne rode them to a second victory and, the following year, at the request of a majority of

riders, all the Tour bikes were fitted with the rims. They gave better braking which meant descending was quicker.

Eddy Merckx, arguably the greatest cyclist of all time, insisted on Mavic rims, although, when he beat the hour record in 1972, he was using a different make. Mavic hailed his triumph, nevertheless: Merckx had proved, once more, that Mavics were 'the rims of champions'. By 1978, they were producing 4000 rims every day, had cornered 65 per cent of the world market and equipped 25 professional teams.

Innovation through painstaking design research and rigorous testing has been the watchword of Mavic's operation from the start. At the same time, their designers and engineers, encouraged by the management's vision, have never been shy of pursuing a line which might not have seemed an obvious commercial winner at the outset. Years of development before manufacture, road testing through volunteers, ideas translated into reality and, if the result doesn't satisfy them, on grounds of safety, foremost, they ditch it, as they did with the Speelo rim, made of moulded thermoplastic and loaded with glass fibre. Produced, finally, in 1980, the rim lacked rigidity and, despite considerable investment, it couldn't be marketed and Mavic called halt. Time, effort, money gone for naught.

In 1979, the company, by now based in Annecy, launched its 'tout Mavic'

Random sampling and checking are used alongside
more formal quality control protocols.

RIGHT

Hub shells are machined from aluminium blanks
in the CNC machine. It goes without saying that
accuracy and structural integrity are built into each
component.

component set: brakes, pedals, chainset, headset, hubs, bars and rims. And bearings. Here, an insight into how they work. 'Spokes were breaking', says one of their engineers, 'and at first we thought the fault lay in the rims. Then we realised that the problem was in the hubs, and that's how we got interested in bearings.'

By this time, they had closed down their advertising campaign completely because they no longer needed routine forms of publicity. During the 1972 Dauphiné-Libéré stage race, Bruno Gormand, son of Henry, loaned his Mavic car to a team manager whose motor had broken down. An idea

sprouted. Since then, the familiar yellow Mavic neutral assistance cars (yellow shows up best on television) have supported most professional races, MTB, BMX, track and triathlon included, and not a few cyclo-touriste events, on the calendar. Mavic thus shows itself in as wide a forum of public view as exists to be what it absolutely insists on for its products: utterly reliable. And, taking everything seriously, they put their support car mechanics and drivers through exacting trials: to begin with, it took 30 seconds from the time a mechanic jumped out of the car to launching the cyclist back on the road. So, they trained in the factory yard and trimmed the time to 15 seconds for a rear wheel, 10 for the front. Now, the support

Research and development, engineering and product realisation take place under one roof. Simple metal hoops are finessed in an endless pursuit of marginal gains, improved performance, better reliability and greater safety.

fleet comprises both cars and motorbikes, which latter were first tested in the 1984 Paris-Roubaix, whose course inhibits the ready access of support vehicles to riders.

The Mavic ethos is rooted in love of cycling – most of the employees ride a bike, many compete and, as a company spokesman says: 'We stand apart in the industrial world because we share a complicity with our customers, we share the same passion.' It's not sentiment, either: you can't make components for racing machines, at any level, unless you have some sense of what it's like to race. Professionals demand the best on offer and, from the strips of metal which arrive in large bundles at the Annecy plant in Saint-Trivier, to the rims into which they are cut, shaped, perforated, sealed, machined, tested, assembled into wheels, every step is monitored and checked with one objective in mind. That objective is summed up in a company promise on a wall-chart detailing the range of bicycle components the Mavic enterprise produces: 'A better bike begins here.'

As we leave the factory, we see a woman standing on a large square of sorbo rubber, fixedly bouncing a wheel rim up and down in slow motion. Is this some kind of Zen exercise in concentration? Therapy for frayed nerves? She is, in fact, shaking out through the spoke holes any crumbs of alu that may be caught inside the rim … a further study in perfection, therefore.

Many professional teams and individual riders have long and close ties to Mavic. The relationship is mutually beneficial: there's effective feedback for Mavic and cutting edge technology for the rider.

ABOVE
After-sales care, repairs and servicing are very important to a company like Mavic. Their products are used (and abused) in some tough environments and occasionally need further attention.

LEFT
Rims and neutral service sit well with the Mavic prefix.

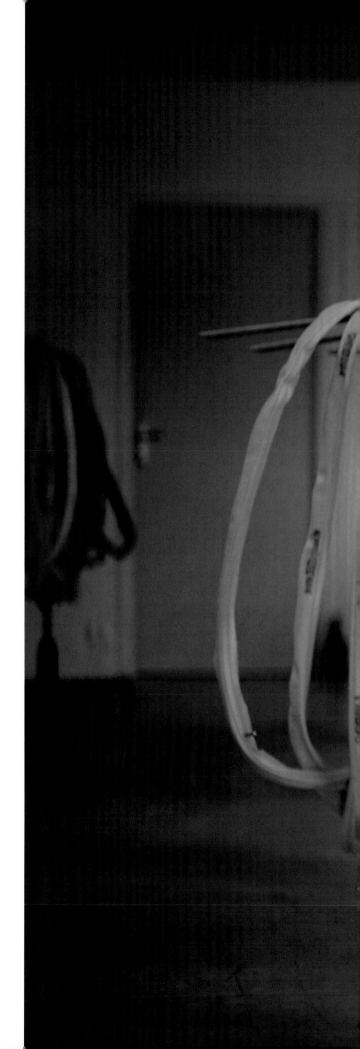

TYRES • Plurien, Brittany, France

This quiet efficient space contrasts with the noisy and chaotic environment into which the product will be pitched.

FMB

The imprimatur of a professional for any product is of inestimable worth. The fact that so many of today's pro riders choose FMB tubulars is immediate testimony to their superior worth and quality. Tom Boonen, one of an elite few to have won the Paris-Rubaix, 'Hell of the North', three times, surely one of the most rigorous tests of a tyre's capacity to stand up to rough treatment, rides on FMB as does another P-R winner, Fabian Cancellara. Taylor Phinney rode FMB track tyres to a rainbow jersey in the individual pursuit at the 2011 Worlds in Denmark and many pro teams choose the tubulars handmade by the last manufacturer of them in France at the small light-filled, airy works in Plurien in Britanny.

François works with his son Renaud and his daughter Aurélie. François, born in 1965, was fired by the Tour victories of the Bernards – Thévenet and Hinault – and won a few modest races but was more drawn to mechanics and making his own tubulars. He went into business administration. In 2005 he quit the humdrum world of the office and started making tubulars. Out of passion. Crazy guy. It worked. He designed and commissioned a sewing machine – the only machine in the works – threaded the needle and set to work in a small garage. He produced his first tub stamped FMB in April 2006 and has since been manufacturing between 130 and 150 of them every month. Each tub takes around one and a half hours to make but the adhesive binding the tread takes as long again to dry.

Some 80 separate processes go into the manufacture of a single tubular which consists of an inner tube made of rubber around which is sewn an outer casing made of cotton or silk onto whose upper surface is glued a strip of rubber tread. FMB buy in the inner tube and the tread strip but they make everything else. The cotton outer casing is marginally heavier and longer-lasting than the silk

Around 80 different steps are needed to make an FMB tubular tyre. It's a slow process because of the drying time that has to be allowed between each step.

A handmade tubular tyre is an amalgam of first rate materials, top grade weaving and exceptional cutting and tailoring skills.

High volume, low rolling resistance, great ride comfort. The FMB casing is an exceptional piece of work.

A born craftsman, Francois always wanted to work with his hands and gave up a conventional job in commerce to work at his sewing machine.

The lightweight latex tube is carefully wrapped and fixed into the casing.

Whichever side of the clincher versus tubular debate you fall on there's no denying the pedigree of the FMB product.

The reputation which FMB have built up is almost exclusively the result of the success of their products. Podium placings and word of mouth beat any advertising.

Cotton, silk and latex are wrapped together in a strong, supple and reliable product. The fine fabric casing along with the high thread count cuts down rolling resistance and cushions the ride. They're a popular choice during the cobbled classics.

Needlework with the quality of haute couture.

It's a real shame that this quality of needlework is going to be hidden under a layer of glue never to see the light of day again until the tyre is ripped off because it is either punctured or worn out.

but cannot stand as high an inflated pressure. The silk, therefore, because of its weight:strength ratio gives maximum performance. Hence the celebrated FMB Roubaix silk tubular*.

All the tubulars are stamped FMB and, though he may give a few away to amateur riders, to encourage them, he does not sponsor anyone. It's too expensive and, in truth, the publicity he gets through the high visibility of FMB on winning tyres is enough to keep the family trio hard at work. A professional team will order 60-80 tubulars for Paris-Roubaix and a similar quantity for the Tour de France time trials. That's around ten per rider.

He articulates why professionals ride FMB. 'Performance, comfort, safety. A light, flexible casing gives peerless grip on the road and the faster you ride the more you feel the advantages of the tub. And, tubs with higher sidewalls can absorb and cushion shocks more readily.' The material shell of an FMB has a finer density than that of a vulcanised tub. It's more flexible and consumes less energy. Moreover, because it deflates so much less readily, it will always provide a cushion between the rider and the tarmac – even when punctured a tub will still function efficiently enough for quite some time.

The FMB cotton casing is built up in a slow process from one thread spooling off a reel. (Other makers use three threads simultaneously.) François Marie varies the diameter of the cross-section and the density of the texture and can add anti-puncture reinforcement, although this adds weight and reduces the performance. 'For Paris-Roubaix we stick 0.2mm sheets of latex on the sidewall which is where most punctures are sustained on the cobbles.'

Working at a granite-topped bench, François Marie is phlegmatic about the future. A modest expansion of the work force – another seamstress, perhaps – a few developments in the range, but, essentially, the core concentration is unchanging. 'I cannot cut my price to compete with other brands', he says, 'because I would lose money. So, we compete on quality.' The point is made. Pro teams continue to use his tubs despite branding obligations to sponsors which may conflict with the appearance of the FMB stamp on the tyres.

Team sponsors exert a powerful hold but some riders are willing to insist on FMB Tubulars when they feel they really need them rather than using their standard issue kit. Tom Boonen and Fabian Cancellara are two high profile examples.

*Kevlar has been used: it's tough and resistant to puncturing but uncomfortable to ride and eats up energy. Polyester has been tried, too, but it stretches under high pressure and nullifies the benefit of the tubular.

BELOW LEFT
A little adhesive in the form of a latex solution is applied to the porous tubular casing prior to folding the ends, adding the inner tube and sewing it all up into the tyre.

BELOW RIGHT
Using a straight edge while folding the edges of the casing together. This will eventually form the machine-stitched seam onto which the tape is finally secured.

The tread, something which is not made in house, is lined up with the casing and carefully seated.

Francois is a perfectionist. His eye is his metrology, his quality control.

TYRES • Korbach, Germany

The Continental factory in Korbach makes tyres.
Lots of them.

CONTINENTAL

Founded, with Germanic precision, on 8 October 1871, the Continental-Caoutchouc-und Gutta Percha* Compagnie of Hanover, in Saxony, first produced soft rubber products, rubberised fabrics and solid bicycle and carriage tyres. Clinging to the more traditional form of transport which it supplied, the company adopted a rampant horse as its trademark.

In 1892, however, Continental became the first company in Germany to manufacture pneumatic tyres for bicycles and, shortly after that, tyres for the newly invented automobile. In 1900, Continental provided the sealant for the gas bags on the first German airship and the emphatic victory of the first Daimler car to be called Mercedes on Continental pneumatic tyres in the 1901 Nice-Salon-Nice rally gave the firm marked stature. Hitherto, car tyres had no pattern on the treads. With an eye to the commercial potential of conspicuous branding, Continental introduced their own unique pattern of tread in 1905 and were soon producing riveted non-skid tyres to fit to cars competing in the new craze – motor racing and long-distance rallies on the still primitive roads of Europe. Technical innovation, the development of new materials, high-profile successes in motor sport established Continental as a prime manufacturer of tyres and various other products, including a rubber-metal bonding, registered as Schwingmetall, applied as absorbers for damping engine vibrations and noise. Gradually, the company concentrated on tyre manufacture alone and devoted much ingenuity

*Why it used the French word (from the Peruvian) for rubber rather than the German 'Gummi' (originally Latin for the secretion of the Arabian acacia, ie gum) is not clear. Gutta Percha is the Malayan equivalent.

ABOVE
The carcasses for high end clinchers are made from a mixture of nylon and rubber. The exact specification of the mix depends on the type of tyre, but can be adjusted to add specific characteristics such as grip and durability.

LEFT
Spools of treated nylon used in the manufacture of tubular casings.

The Competition tubular is described by Continental as being 'premier class' and the 'grand master' of tyres. It's also an example of astonishingly neat needlework.

Can a factory as large as this one still claim to make things by hand? We think that it can.

Like all tubular tyres these ones have to wait their turn to be sewn up.

The technology within a tyre can easily be overlooked but something like anti-puncture technology can mean the difference between a ride and a great ride. Vectran is a reinforced polymer layer and sits under the tread to ward off tacks, thorns and other such hazards.

Many of the production steps take place with the tyre carcass mounted on an expanding drum. This keeps a tension in the carcass which means the tyres end up nice and straight once they've been cured in the mould.

and research into advancing the technology. Always its driving ethos: Handmade in Germany.

Dazzling success on the Formula One tracks consolidated the company's standing but its manufacture of bicycle tyres continued and now the company makes what many cyclists, professional and amateur, regard as the best tubulars suited to the climate and roads of northern Europe – better grip in the wet, hardier on rugged surfaces, more tolerant of the cold. Why, you may ask, is such a giant of manufacture included in this book, with its slant on handbuilt components? Because the Continental tubs are still made by hand, in a small factory in Korbach, in Hessen, central Germany, near the Rothaargebirge mountain chain, to which part of the operation moved from Hanover in 1971. They supply around 2000 tubs (and clinchers for training) to professional riders every year. The feedback from pros is vital to the Continental team. They report on abrasion, rolling resistance, susceptibility to puncture … time triallists, in particular, who have a refined sensitivity to variations in speed and the way tyres react to surges in power and handling on corners, give important information on the quality of the tyres they are using. Such data taken in conjunction with laboratory testing is vital to improvement of the tyre. When Continental first started supplying the Italian pro team Mercatone Uno with tyres, the team mechanics had been in the habit of changing the riders' tyres every day. That was no longer necessary with the tougher Continental rubber which did not need to be changed more than once a week.

The casing of the Continental tub, fabric and a thin rubber coating, is squeezed through large steel rollers and the rubber coating is pressed into the meshed fibres of the fabric. The process is repeated with a second coating of rubber, heated to soften it and facilitate the bonding. The tread is introduced by a heating mould. Now begins the hand work.

The rubber is still sticky and the intricate job of stitching the casing cannot be done by machine. Nimble fingers sew the casing into its final tubular shape with red thread, after which another handworker applies, first, a latex emulsion coating round the inner circumference of the tyre, second a base tape, sealed with heat.

Four gold, four silver and three bronze medals at the 2012 Worlds Road Races in the Netherlands on Continental tyres … Women's World Champion Downhill on Continental Mud King tyres … a shower of medals at the London Olympics … Deutsche Technik seit 1871.

The tread and carcass are joined together ready for the heat process in the mould.

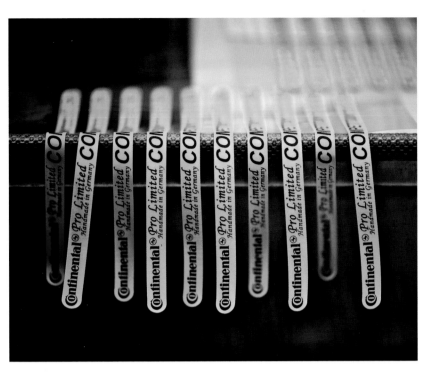

TOP
Product identification like this doesn't make the tyre go any faster or last any longer or even allow you to go deeper into corners but it is vital for sponsorship and brand recognition. Fixing on the stickers is treated with as much care as all of the other processes.

ABOVE AND RIGHT
A laser line guides the sticker into the right place.

Vulcanisation takes place at 180°C for three minutes. All parts of the tyre, the carcass, tread and bead are joined during this process and the tread pattern is formed at the same time.

Bladders force the tyre into the mould with steam. Any excess rubber from the tread leaks from little escape holes to be trimmed or more likely worn off later. These tell-tale little hairs are called sprues.

One of the moulds. This sector of the factory is very hot.

ABOVE
Clincher tyres are often seen as playing second fiddle to the more elite tubulars seen in the pro peloton but millions of cyclists appreciate these high quality Korbach offerings.

RIGHT
Sharp eyes and nimble fingers are prerequisites on this production line.

CARBON TUBING AND FRAMES
• Vaulx-Milieu, Rhône-Alps, France

Weaving their own carbon tubes is one of the things which makes Time bicycles different from their competitors. It's slow and expensive. Vive la différence.

TIME

Time is based just outside Lyon, France's third city, which occupies a strategic position dominating the valleys of the Rhône and Saône. To the east lies the great natural barrier of the Alps and Lyon acts, therefore, as a gateway to the mountains which form one of the most important battlefields of the Tour de France. Lyon, at the conjunction of two arterial rivers on the north-south axis and at a crossroads for traffic entering France from both east and west, was, from its beginnings, an important entrepôt for all manner of trade. Its principal industry, the manufacture of silk, has its modern counterpart in the production of synthetic fibres, for which Lyon has become well-known. It is, therefore, part of Time's contribution to a timeless succession of manufacturing excellence that Lyon is its home, a town named for an ancient Celtic god, Lugus, meaning 'Light'.

Time is celebrated for extremely high production values. Luxe is the word they use, de luxe, conspicuous high quality, very expensive, with a disdain for false economies that would have pleased a Borgia. Their range of products is quite small – frames, pedals, handlebars, bar stems and bottle cages – but the constant refinement of everything they make, through incessant, tireless research and development, is dedicated to the twin demands of lightness and strength. They lay unique claim to the process of Resin Transfer Moulding of carbon fibre. Simply put, carbon fibre is placed in two halves of a mould, the mould is closed up and resin is injected into the mould.

Carbon, Vectran, polyamide and Kevlar are incorporated into the weave to add more or less of qualities such as stiffness, vibration damping and compliance. Each thread is very thin yet very strong.

Comparisons to a spider's web are easy to make but also quite apt. The weave looks complex but is actually quite simple. It looks fragile but is surprisingly strong.

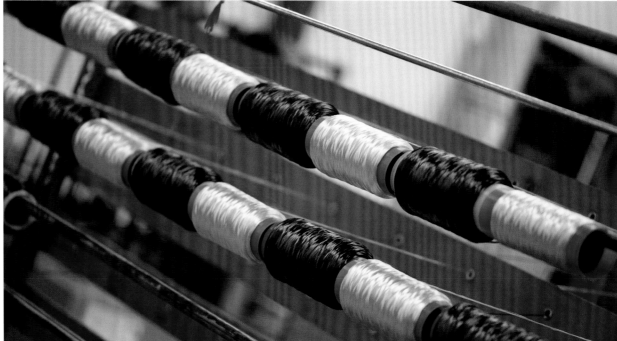

Even the angle of the weave can be adjusted to suit whatever Time require.

The end product. Flattened by a roller before the drop into the box ready for the cutting and placing.

TOP
Once the sock has come from the loom it is cut to size and layered onto wax tube formers – the skeleton – and steel mandrels to give the basic shape.

ABOVE
The layers of carbon are built up on the formers depending on the size of the frame and the particular area.

LEFT
This is the scale of one of the weaving machines. It's a painstaking process but well worth it in the end. Each of the bobbins jigs and clatters around at a rate of knots.

Time frames are renowned as probably the lightest bikes on the market but endowed with a resistant strength seemingly at odds with the airy thinness of their structure. A number of professional road and mountain bike teams use Time frames with their distinctive integral seat tube.

Time eschews the common pre-peg carbon fibre technology and deploys what might seem to be a somewhat homespun process. It is, in fact, very high-tech. In the weaving room bobbins of thread clatter and spin, a noise reminiscent of an old textile mill, as they feed individual fibres of Kevlar, Vectran and carbon into a sock that will eventually form the tubes of the bicycle frame or handlebars. The process is fiddly, slow and closely gauged as the web of gossamer threads is funnelled into the loom and onwards to a decidedly low-tech cardboard box. These 'socks' are then cut to size and fitted over blanks, forms and wax shapes before they are taken and fitted into a mould which is in turn baked under extreme pressure as resin is injected onto the fibres. The wax shapes are lost but their shape remains.

PEDALS

Early Tour riders complained of many physical discomforts associated with the brutal challenge of covering vast distances on poor roads, not least among the hazards, the loss of toenails. Their shoes, generally of soft leather, gave their feet little support and, crammed into the confined cage of the toe clips and strapped tight to reduce movement, the unprotected feet suffered accordingly. Long hours of extended riding, maybe in bitter cold, driving rain, extremes of heat, acted cruelly on the poor toes. Had no one thought to fit the clipless pedals invented way back in 1895 when the American Charles Hanson, of Peace Dale, Rhode Island, came up with a pedal which, by twisting, locked into a fixture on the pedal and came free by untwisting. Simple. Improvements on the design ensued and then … someone came up with the toe strap and clipless pedals vanished. Like the Cheshire Cat, leaving its grin behind.

Almost a century passed before an astute mind made the comparison between the quick-release fastenings on a ski boot and the possibility of a clipless pedal for cyclists. Photographs of riders pitched off in a crash, their feet still locked into the toe clip add to the sense of horror any cyclist feels in contemplation of a prang at high speed. In 1987, Time Sport International came into being, a name forever associated with the high-tech clipless pedal. It seems a small claim to sporting distinction that Time

Strands of fibre are used to tie the socks of carbon onto the mandrels. Still very floppy though the frame shape is at least recognisable.

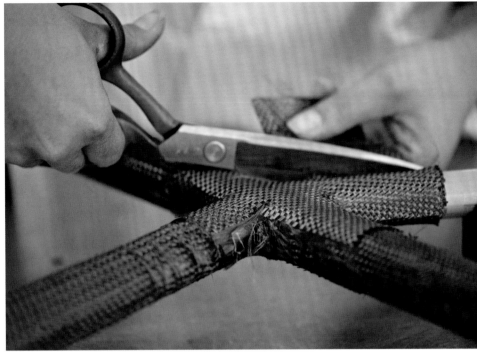

TOP LEFT
Extra carbon is applied to high stress areas such as the seat mast and the bottom bracket. A hot air gun softens the fibres allowing them to fit more closely together.

TOP RIGHT
In a world obsessed by weight any excess is carefully trimmed to leave just enough to do the job. No more, no less.

LEFT
The mould containing the carbon is made ready for the RTM process. It's a carefully controlled and precise operation but Time, along with Airbus, Boeing, Lamborghini and Ferrari, believe that it's worth the effort.

Awaiting its fate, the bottom bracket shell sits in the line for the RTM process. A couple of hours will see this soft and flexible package transformed into hard and rigid frame part.

should vaunt its contribution to victories in the Grande Boucle to an apparently minor item of bicycle componentry which had dispensed with the binding strap and buckle, but its list of champions who have ridden to their victories on Time pedals is impressive. Perhaps most telling, the fact that the double winner of the Paris-Roubaix (in 1992-3), Gilbert Duclos-Lasalle, was using their pedals. On that most unforgiving of courses, bike and rider take a relentless hammering. Riders all but expect to come off – cobbles, ruts, slicks of gluey mud, blinding dust, the jostling of other men trying to stay upright or find a better line add to the overall stress of a hard race. To know that if you do come off, at least your feet will not stay clamped to the machine and you have some chance of avoiding the worst of a crash is something.

LEFT
The proprietary moulds are big, heavy and super accurate. The same high quality frame can be repeated time after time.

LEFT
The front end of the bike and the rear triangle are secured in a jig ready for bonding and the fitting of dropouts.

BELOW
Sanding and rubbing down are part of an intensive finishing process.

ABOVE
A detail of the bottom bracket shell before bonding into the rear triangle.

LEFT
Hot off the press and oven fresh. A brand new Time frame about to have the excess resin from the mould chipped away.

CONTACTS

Alex Singer – http://www.cycles-alex-singer.fr/

Ben Serotta – http://serotta.com/

Breadwinner – http://breadwinnercycles.com/

Brian Rourke – http://www.brianrourke.co.uk/

Brooks Saddles – http://www.brooksengland.com/

Chris King – http://chrisking.com/

Cinelli – http://www.cinelli.it/

Columbus – http://www.columbustubi.com/

Continental – http://www.conti-tyres.co.uk/conticycle/

Cyfac – http://www.cyfac.fr/

Faggin – http://www.fagginbikes.com/index.php?lang=en

FMB – http://www.fmbtires.com/

Guru – http://www.gurucycles.com/en

Independent Fabrication – http://www.ifbikes.com/

Ira Ryan – http://www.iraryancycles.com/

Mark DiNucci – http://www.dinuccicycles.com/DINUCCI-CYCLES

Mavic – http://www.mavic.com/en

Paris Cycles – http://www.condorcycles.com/paris/paris.html

Pegoretti – http://www.pegoretticicli.com/

Reynolds Tubing – http://reynoldstechnology.biz/

Richard Sachs – http://www.richardsachs.com/

Roberts Cycles – http://www.robertscycles.com/

Royce – http://www.royceuk.co.uk

Sapim – http://www.sapim.be

Selle Italia – http://www.selleitalia.com/se_it3/

Seven Cycles – http://www.sevencycles.com/

Spécialités TA – http://www.specialites-ta.com/

Time – http://www.time-sport.com/

Tony Pereira – http://www.pereiracycles.com/

United Bicycle Institute – http://www.bikeschool.com/

Winter Bicycles – http://www.winterbicycles.com/

INDEX